Russell Wilson: The Inspiring Story of One of Football's Greatest Quarterbacks

An Unauthorized Biography

By: Clayton Geoffreys

Visit my website at www.claytongeoffreys.com
Cover photo by Larry Maurer is licensed under CC BY 2.0 / modified from original

Table of Contents

Foreword

Few quarterbacks enter the league and have as immediate of an impact on their franchise as Russell Wilson has had with the Seattle Seahawks. Already a Super Bowl Champion in his early twenties, Russell Wilson has an exciting NFL career ahead of him. It's been a fascinating ride in terms of Russell's journey into becoming a professional football player, when at one point he was just a two-star recruit out of high school. Thank you for downloading *Russell Wilson: The Inspiring Story of One of Football's Greatest Quarterbacks*. In this unauthorized biography, we will learn about Russell Wilson's incredible life story and impact on the game of football. Hope you enjoy and if you do, please do not forget to leave a review! Also, check out my website at claytongeoffreys.com to join my exclusive list where I let you know about my latest books and give you goodies!

Cheers,

Clayton Geoffreys

Visit me at www.claytongeoffreys.com

Introduction

There is no doubt that Russell Wilson is one of the best quarterbacks in the game today. In just his second season as the starting quarterback for the Seattle Seahawks, Russell Wilson took them to a dominating Super Bowl victory. While his discipline and dedication toward the sport have led him to where he is today, Russell Wilson graciously gives credit to his father for teaching him everything he needed to become what he is today. In fact, he is rooted in sports through his family. His grandfather, Harrison B. Wilson Jr., played college basketball and football at Kentucky State University; his father, Harrison Wilson III, also played college football and basketball, and was with the San Diego Chargers for one preseason before being released.

Dedication and a little luck played significant roles in making Russell Wilson the player he is. He committed himself to being a talented athlete because he always loved sports and has an extremely competitive spirit. He also had a little luck play its part because he is genetically gifted and was born into a family that loves competition.

As a result, Russell Wilson was able to take his athleticism to the next level. His dedication to what he does is also deeply rooted in his strong religious values. He is known for being a devout Christian, often mentioning his faith and thanking God during his press conferences. By having a dedicated father, who taught him everything he needed to know about sports, and his personal dedication, high work ethic, and strong religious beliefs, Russell Wilson learned everything it takes to be a successful quarterback in the NFL.

Russell is recognized by many of his co-players and coaches as one of the most competitive players on the whole Seattle Seahawks team. While most quarterbacks have an average height of 6'4", allowing them better visibility of the entire field, Russell is one of the shortest NFL players today, at only 5'11". However, despite having a height disadvantage, Russell's competitive spirit and dedication to becoming one of the best quarterbacks in the league have allowed him to take on a leading role that most critics would have said he was incapable of achieving.

By leading the Seahawks to 36 wins, Russell Wilson set the record for most wins ever as a starting quarterback in his first three seasons. He outperformed other starting quarterbacks such as Dan Marino, Matt Ryan, and Andrew Luck. They each had 33 wins in their first three seasons.

Russell Wilson has achieved several remarkable goals in his four-year NFL career. He is one of three quarterbacks to throw 50 or more touchdown passes in their first two seasons (Dan Marino and Peyton Manning are the other two). He is one of two quarterbacks to throw over 50 touchdowns and also rush for more than 1,000 yards in the span of two seasons. Russell Wilson has also been able to keep his team close. He had lost just one game by double digits since 2010, the time when he played college football. That sole loss was to the Green Bay Packers, 27-17, in Week 2 of the 2015 NFL season. Indeed, Russell is an amazing quarterback and is already breaking records after his third season in the NFL.

Wilson has already gone to the Super Bowl twice in his first four years in the NFL. He led the Seahawks to their first-ever Vince Lombardi Trophy in Super Bowl XLVIII.

Russell is not even close to being in his prime, which NFL quarterbacks reach in their late 20s and early 30s. For this reason, Wilson is a quarterback that fans will be keeping an eye on. As he continues to gain more experience and more victories playing in the most competitive football league in the world, he is likely to be elected to the Pro Football Hall of Fame in Canton, Ohio. Among the best quarterbacks in the NFL today are Aaron Rodgers, Tom Brady, Drew Brees and Ben Roethlisberger, just to name a few. However, these quarterbacks are all over 30 years of age already, and they will probably be retiring soon. Besides Andrew Luck, Russell Wilson is one of the few young quarterbacks that many will be keeping a keen eye on.

In addition to football, Wilson is also a talented baseball player. The Colorado Rockies drafted him in 2010. And while he is currently dedicated solely to football, he has been showing some interest in competing in Major League Baseball as well.

So what lies in the future for Russell Wilson? He says that he is excited to continue playing football and coming out as one of the best, but he still has the heart to start a career as a professional baseball player. Indeed, his love and dedication to competing in sports will make him one of the most highly anticipated players of his time. He is 100% dedicated to playing whatever competitive sport he decides to try, and fans around the world are extremely excited to see what is next for this superstar athlete.

In the remaining chapters of this book, you will learn about Wilson's childhood life, his high school and college career as a quarterback, and his outstanding NFL career. We will also take a look at Russell Wilson's personal life and aspirations. So, if you would like to learn more about the life of Russell Wilson, please read on.

Chapter 1: Childhood and Early Life

Russell Wilson was born in Cincinnati, Ohio, on November 29, 1988. He and his family lived in a 2,190-square-foot, four-bedroom house in the Springfield Township area. Before moving into this house, the Wilsons lived in an apartment five miles away in the North College Hill area.

They sold their Springfield Township home on July 18, 1990. Wilson was less than 2 years old at the time.

For most of his childhood life, Wilson grew up in Richmond, Virginia. Wilson has an older brother and sister. Although his ancestry is primarily African-American, he also has some Native American in his ethnic background. His great-great-grandfather was a slave, but he was freed after the North won the Civil War.

Wilson grew up in a competitive atmosphere not only in sports but also in education. Both of Wilson's parents had professional careers—his father, Harrison Benjamin Wilson III, was a lawyer, and his mother, Tammy Wilson, worked as a legal nurse consultant. Being a competitive athlete was also in his family's blood. His father was a split end for Dartmouth College. After attending law school, Wilson's father tried out for the San Diego Chargers in 1980 and played during the preseason. He was later let go but was not concerned about it, as he then turned toward becoming a successful lawyer.

Russell Wilson's grandfather was also highly competitive in both education and sports. He was a former president of Norfolk State University, and played basketball and baseball for Kentucky State University. Russell's brother, Harry, also played football and baseball at the University of Richmond.

Growing up in a family that wanted to achieve greatness in education, career life, and even in athletics, had a tremendous impact on the person he is—a Seattle Seahawks Super Bowl champion after playing his second season in the NFL.

He reveals that his dinner conversations with his family had a profound impact on him and his siblings. Every night, they would talk about faith, family, and education. They also discussed role models such as Martin Luther King Jr. and Derek Jeter. Those were the kind of people Harrison Wilson III and Tammy Wilson wanted their children to emulate.

Wilson has an older brother named Harry (born 1985). Having someone like him, who was highly competitive in sports, also contributed toward Russell's success. The two brothers always played sports together and were highly competitive when they challenged each other.

Wilson also has a younger sister named Anna, who is 18 years old. She, too, is into sports. Anna Wilson is a 5'8" guard who starred in basketball at Bellevue, Washington, High School. She averaged 20.6 points, 4.5 assists and 5.7 steals per game as a senior.

She has committed to play for the Stanford Cardinal beginning in the 2016 NCAA women's basketball season.

The Wilson family is extremely religious, and Russell Wilson still holds onto these beliefs today. He became a devout Christian at the early age of 14 after he claims he had a dream where he saw Jesus.

More specifically, Wilson envisioned his father having just passed away. Jesus then entered the room and invited the younger Wilson to know him better. The latter went to church that week and had been a devout Christian since then.

Before his conversion, Wilson claims he was a "bad kid."

As a matter of fact, he said he had a lot of pent-up anger when he was a young boy. This was a far cry from the Russell Wilson we know now.

Wilson said, "I used to beat people up. Truthfully, I used to beat people up a lot. Many of you readers probably think I have been Mr. Goody Two-Shoes my whole life, but honestly, I was a bully growing up.

"In elementary and middle school, I threw kids against the wall. I rubbed their heads in the dirt at recess. I bit them. I even knocked their teeth out.

"I had a lot of anger that I didn't know what to do with."

Wilson has turned things around since he made his commitment to Jesus Christ.

Even as a child, he showed the persona of a competitive person and a leader. He always loved to play sports whenever he had free time. Wilson's third-grade teacher recalled how Wilson would often play sports during recess and would play even when his school did not allow them to go outside because it was raining.

Wilson's mother Tammy recalls that the teachers said he was always leading other kids to play competitive sports, even if they had to play inside. His mother described a time during a recess break at Wilson's school in which the students were required to stay indoors due to rain. Wilson sat in a rocking chair and gathered all of the kids together to play an indoor sport that he made up. He would lead and direct the entire event. Tammy, Wilson's mother, believed that even at that time he already had a leadership persona about him. It's safe to say his family ingrained his competitive drive and determination.

Mrs. Wilson said, "I always knew he was going to do something great, something special because he's a special kid."

Because Wilson's brother, Harry Russell IV, was three years older than he, Russell always had a hard time beating him in any sport. Harry would never go easy on his younger brother. Tammy recalled times when the younger Wilson would complain about how his brother was cheating in some way. However, when she would tell him that he probably should not play against Harry if he did not like how his older brother was playing, Wilson simply could not do that. He loved to compete and could not consider doing something different.

"Russell couldn't beat Harry," Mrs. Wilson said. "And he'd come inside and say, 'Mom, mom, Harry's doing such and such,' and I'd say, 'Russell, if you can't handle it, then maybe you need to stay inside.'

"He'd pout, 'No, no, no, I'm going back out there.' I think his brother really helped him to be tough because Harry just wouldn't let him win."

The brothers loved playing basketball together. And, of course, there was football.

Because Harry played wide receiver, Russell took on the role of quarterback. They spent countless hours throwing the football to one another. As a result, Russell Wilson developed two things he was known for even at a young age: arm strength and accuracy.

Perhaps the first to discover Wilson's future as a football player was former Collegiate School (Richmond, Va.) football coach Charlie McFall.

Wilson was the ball boy for the high school team. Harry was a member of that squad. His younger brother was still in grade school. During a break in the action, Russell threw the football to an official with such velocity it impressed McFall.

"I'm going to stick around for that kid," he said to himself.

Wilson was in sixth grade when he first played organized football. His baseball coach asked him to dress up for a football game against the Tuckahoe Tomahawks.

Wilson describes what happened next.

"On the very first play, our starting quarterback got knocked out of the game," he says. "The coach sent me in to play quarterback. I told him, 'I don't know any of the plays.' He just told me to do the best I could.

"Well, I drew plays in the grass and just improvised my way through. I ended up throwing six touchdown passes, and we won by 45 points."

While Wilson wanted to spend every extra moment he had playing sports, his parents never let him think that his education was less important. They made sure he knew that he needed to take his education very seriously. His mother helped him with science and math while his father helped him with English and history.

However, education was not Wilson's biggest priority. He was simply more focused on his love for sports. In school, it was more about being competitive in whatever sport he was in, as well as socializing with his peers. These were ultimately two crucial qualities that Wilson harnessed, which likely made him become such a great NFL quarterback today.

Around the seventh grade, Tammy recalls how her son would leverage his education through socializing and sports. He would find students that were smarter than him academically, and would make deals for them to help him with his homework and studies while he taught them how to improve in sports.

However, there is simply no greater influence in Russell Wilson's life than his father, Harrison Wilson III. Harrison was not only responsible for Wilson's love for sports, but also in teaching his son how to have a strong work ethic, discipline, and dedication toward playing competitively. Harrison would take sports to the next level for Russell and his brother, not just by talking about their current involvement in sports, but also by talking to them about everything they should know if and when they played professionally. He instilled into their minds that what they practiced and used then would allow them to play professionally. He talked about everything in detail, including their salaries and lives as future NFL players. Harrison Wilson III even required his sons to write post-game speeches that they would give if they were to win the Super Bowl.

He also talked about how they needed to be well-groomed and dressed whenever meeting with the press, which is why Wilson always is adamant today about taking a shower and dressing up after every game before he goes out and speaks to the press.

Russell Wilson and his brother Harry even used to play with a football their father caught from former San Diego Chargers quarterback Dan Fouts. At a young age, Wilson already envisioned he was Steve Young or Warren Moon.

Even today, Russell Wilson realizes that his love for the sport and his ability to make it into the NFL was primarily due to his father. And while his father passed away due to diabetes complications in 2010, Wilson never forgets that it was his father's dedication and love that gave him that drive toward becoming a professional quarterback.

Wilson said, "I play with my dad in my heart every game because he really taught me about discipline, preparation, and how to be an ultimate competitor."

Weldon Bradshaw, an English teacher at Collegiate School, says the impact of Wilson's father on Russell is very apparent.

"You see the influence he's had on him," says Bradshaw. "Russell has taken the high road, but you see where he got the training for that."

For his part, Seattle Coach Pete Carroll recognizes that Wilson's outstanding leadership qualities come from his father. Carroll said, "Russell is a great leader. His dad was a really, really extraordinary positive factor in Russell's life and still lives in his heart daily. His dad was a great part of his makeup."

Chapter 2: High School Years

Russell Wilson attended Collegiate School in Richmond, Virginia, which is a private preparatory school for boys and girls. Collegiate focuses on helping each and every student realize his own unique talents and gifts. It also focuses on teaching students how to become responsible citizens.

Wilson's success today is based on his high school experience. He was not only the football team's starting quarterback, but he also played baseball. However, his achievements were primarily attained on the football field, as one of the best quarterbacks of all time at Collegiate.

Wilson started playing for his high school baseball team when he was only in the eighth grade. Even back then, he was known for having charming charisma and an uncanny devotion toward playing sports professionally—something that you would rarely see in a child that age.

Wilson's head coach at that time was Charlie McFall, the Cougars' head football coach from 1986 to 2006. One common question he gets about Wilson was whether he was surprised by the boy's current accomplishments.

McFall was never even slightly surprised, as he always saw a competitive spirit within Wilson. He could tell that Wilson, even from an early age, was dedicated to playing at least one sport professionally in the future. McFall mentioned a time when Russell was still a ball boy. Wilson was in the sixth grade then and he could throw a perfect spiral, which amazed everyone who witnessed it.

McFall also told college coaches who scouted Wilson that his quarterback was exceptional both as a player and a person. He told them that even opposing high school coaches would say the same thing about Wilson.

In fact, many knew during his high school career that Russell Wilson was destined for success. His athletic work ethic has always been amazing. By everyone's standards, he was known for always being an overachiever who wanted to take his team and his performance to the next level.

Despite Wilson's lofty status as the Cougars' starting quarterback, he wasn't going to settle for just being good.

Will O'Brien is the current associate athletics director of Collegiate School. In 2005, he applied for the strength coach position. Wilson happened to be a member of the student panel that interviewed O'Brien.

The aspiring strength coach couldn't believe what he heard from Wilson. The quarterback kept asking him how he could get better on the field.

"I remember, and none of the ADs told me who this kid is," O'Brien says. "But I distinctly remember this young man leaning over the table, and he had more questions than anyone else.

"It was like, 'Hey, how do I get faster? How do I get stronger? I'm a baseball player and a quarterback. What are the things that I need to do to get better?'"

Russell was known for taking teams to the next level because, no matter what sport he was playing, he was always looking to succeed. He had that sense of athletic charisma that would inspire the entire team to play at their highest level.

Wilson was not just determined. He was also versatile. He proved this when he played three sports in high school. Aside from football, he also starred in baseball and basketball. Wilson played point guard for Collegiate School head basketball coach Alex Peavey.

High School Football

Russell Wilson started as Collegiate's quarterback in 2005, in his junior year. During his first season, he had 3,287 passing yards and threw 40 touchdown passes. In addition, he rushed for 634 yards and scored 15 rushing touchdowns. For these achievements, he was named all-district, all-region, and all-state player.

The Richmond Times-Dispatch named him its Player of the Year in 2005. He led the Cougars to an unblemished 11-0 record. With him behind center, they won their third straight state title.

When asked to comment, Wilson said, "Not losing much is a great privilege."

He adds there are "critics everywhere." Because of this, he tried to be at his best against the better teams. He said he and his teammates loved the challenge.

When Wilson won *The Richmond Times-Dispatch* Player of the Year honors, McFall praised the junior quarterback for shining on a team dominated by seniors. The Cougars' head football coach cited Wilson's outstanding leadership abilities, saying that he simply made everyone around him better. McFall also lauded Wilson's confidence and knowledge of the game of football.

In 2005, McFall said that Collegiate School resorted to an air-oriented attack more than ever. He considered the team fortunate to have wide receivers who could make big plays at the right time. Despite the Cougars' offensive line being just average, Wilson gave his linemen enough confidence to exceed everyone's expectations.

In 2006, Wilson's senior year, he threw for 3,009 yards and 34 touchdowns and also rushed for 1,132 yards and 18 touchdowns. After achieving these stats, he was again named all-district, all-region, and all-state player. He led his team to the state championship. Because of his accomplishments, he was featured in *Sports Illustrated.*

Aside from his on-field accomplishments, Wilson was elected the president of his senior class in 2006. He graduated from Collegiate School the following year.

The National Football League (NFL) gave a golden commemorative football to Collegiate School in January 2016, almost nine years after Wilson graduated. The football honors the school for developing Wilson during his stay. The NFL gives this to the school of every player and coach who has been active with a Super Bowl team.

The league also gave Collegiate School a new character education curriculum and the opportunity to apply for grants that can help develop their football programs.

College Recruitment

McFall remembers when Wilson's junior year ended. He encouraged his quarterback to list the schools he wanted to attend when he reached the college level. Afterward, he also told Wilson he could attend one-day camps that those particular schools hosted during the summer. The idea was for them to get a sense of how well he played quarterback and how he fit into their system.

The Cougars coach told Wilson this was a much better way to get college coaches and scouts to notice him. He felt that visiting different universities was just a waste of time and money.

McFall also said that Wilson wanted to go to college near the Richmond area so he could be close to his family. At the time, Harrison Wilson III's health was already declining.

Wilson had already visited the University of Virginia and Virginia Tech University. Both the Cavaliers and Hokies were interested. However, they wanted Wilson to play another position. Both schools were eyeing him as a defensive back.

The reason was simple: They had other high-profile quarterbacks on their radar. The Cavaliers wanted four-star prospect Peter Lalich, a 6'3", 235-pound quarterback ranked 11th overall at his position in 2007. The feeling was mutual, so Lalich committed to Virginia.

On the other hand, Hokies head football coach Frank Beamer wanted to sign five-star prospect Tyrod Taylor, who eventually did sign with Virginia Tech. He is currently the Buffalo Bills' starting quarterback.

Because Wilson wasn't having success with Virginia schools, he decided to broaden his horizon. He added four ACC schools to his list. These were Duke University, the University of North Carolina, North Carolina State University, and Wake Forest University.

The North Carolina Tar Heels liked Wilson. Frank Cignetti (currently the quarterbacks coach of the New York Giants) was their offensive coordinator at the time. He tried to convince head football coach John Bunting to take a chance on Wilson. To Cignetti's dismay, North Carolina committed to four-star prospect Mike Paulus. Bunting was hesitant to add another quarterback, as it might cause Paulus to back out.

Wilson then set his sights on North Carolina's fierce cross-town rival, the Duke Blue Devils. He impressed head football coach Ted Roof and his staff so much they wanted to sign him right there and then.

However, Cignetti had also referred Wilson to his brother, Curt, who was the North Carolina State Wolfpack's recruiting coordinator. Curt Cignetti was awestruck at watching Wilson. He reminded him of former Wolfpack standout Philip Rivers, who has made a name for himself with the San Diego Chargers.

Cignetti believed Wilson's agility, decision making, and leadership traits were similar to Rivers'. Marc Trestman, the Wolfpack's quarterbacks coach, also fell in love with Wilson's skills.

The Collegiate School standout also worked out with the Wake Forest Demon Deacons. That went well, just like the others. But, for some reason, the Demon Deacons lost contact with Wilson.

North Carolina State head football coach Chuck Amato and his staff quickly pounced on the opportunity. They, too, were willing to sign Wilson on the spot. Now, he had to choose between North Carolina State and Duke.

The clincher proved to be Wilson's visit to North Carolina State with his parents. Wilson committed to the Wolfpack just before his senior season at Collegiate School.

Nine years after Amato showed his confidence in Wilson, the latter paid him a tribute during his Russell Wilson Passing Academy camp in Raleigh, N.C. When Amato dropped by, he took the opportunity to tell his campers how he made an impact on his life.

"There were other five-star recruits here," the star quarterback said. "I don't know where they are now, they're at home, but (Amato) believed in me."

For his part, Curt Cignetti was impressed not only with Wilson's prowess but also with his family background. He called Wilson "a natural" and also marveled at his ability to play baseball. He adds that Wilson just wanted an opportunity, so they gave him one.

Shortly after Wilson committed to the Wolfpack, they dismissed Amato. They named Tom O'Brien as his replacement. During this time, Cignetti recalls other schools tried to recruit Wilson. He fought hard to keep

Wilson committed. O'Brien had some doubts about the new Wolfpack quarterback because of his height. Cignetti convinced him to give him a chance.

The rest is history.

Chapter 3: College Years at North Carolina State

Russell Wilson started his freshman year at North Carolina State University in 2007. The Wolfpack redshirted Wilson, meaning that he sat on the bench and only participated in practice. However, in the 2008 season, he split time playing quarterback with Daniel Evans, who was a senior, and with junior Harrison Beck. After the fifth week, the other quarterbacks were put on the bench, and Wilson became the starter. The team had 4 wins and 3 losses that season. Russell Wilson continued as the starting quarterback for the remainder of his career at North Carolina State University.

The team went to the PapaJohns.com Bowl game against Rutgers University. Wilson threw for 186 yards and rushed for 46 yards—all before halftime. However, toward the end of the first half, Wilson injured his knee when he was tackled rushing to the 4-yard line. He was forced to sit out the rest of the game. His replacement threw 3 interceptions, and they lost, 29-23. Russell Wilson was named All-ACC first team honors at North Carolina State in 2008, making him the first freshman quarterback to achieve this accomplishment.

In his 2009 season with North Carolina State, Russell Wilson broke of Andre Woodson's record by attempting 379 consecutive passes without an interception. Andre's record was 325 consecutive pass attempts, meaning that Wilson blew his record out of the water. This showed to the football world the dedication and extreme athleticism that Wilson had. To this day, his record has not been broken, and it is highly questionable if anyone will break that record any time soon.

In 2010, Wilson led his team to the Champs Sports Bowl with a record of 9 wins and only 4 losses. North Carolina State defeated West Virginia, 23-7, in that bowl game. After the season, Wilson was named a third-team All-

American by Yahoo Sports. He also finished ninth in the Heisman Trophy voting.

During Wilson's three-year stint with the Wolfpack, he threw for 8,545 yards, with 76 touchdowns and 26 interceptions. He had a 57.8 percent completion rate.

Colorado Rockies and Departure from North Carolina State

The Colorado Rockies selected Wilson in the fourth round of the 2010 MLB draft. They chose him 140th overall. He went to their spring training camp.

"I was blessed enough to play professional baseball," Wilson said. "Get drafted by the Colorado Rockies in the fourth round. I went to spring training and played (single A) ball for several months."

Wilson played second base for Colorado. At 5'11", he considered himself big and fast for that position. He also believes he could run and throw at the Major League level.

Wilson's batting average hovered around the .230 mark during his days in the Rockies' farm system. That and the naysayers' observation he couldn't excel because of his height were his obstacles. Wilson remained unfazed.

The head football coach at North Carolina State, Tom O'Brien, expressed concerns about Wilson's interest in baseball, stating that he should instead focus on his football and baseball career at the college. This conflict between Wilson and O'Brien led to Russell deciding that he should finish his college football career at another school. O'Brien had contacted NFL coaches and general managers to get Wilson an invitation to the 2011 NFL Scouting Combine but was unable to do so. Most likely scouts were concerned about Wilson's height disadvantage. The fact that O'Brien was unable to get Wilson acceptance into the NFL Scouting Combine may have also been a determining factor for Wilson to consider finishing his football career at another school.

O'Brien eventually released Wilson from his North Carolina State scholarship. He named future Tampa Bay Buccaneers quarterback Mike Glennon as his new starter. At the time, Glennon already graduated but still had two years of eligibility left.

O'Brien insists he and Wilson "parted on great terms." He says he made his decision to release the star quarterback based on the facts he had back then.

"It's a great opportunity," says O'Brien. "It was a great opportunity for Russell, and it was a great opportunity for Michael. We were lucky to have those kids the four years we had them playing, five years. People ought to be happy about that."

In 2014, O'Brien told ESPN he and Wilson have been keeping in touch via text message. The former even jokingly asked the current NFL star for tickets.

Wisconsin Badgers

Russell Wilson finished his college football career and college education with the Wisconsin Badgers football team. The head coach for the Badgers, Bret Bielema, announced the welcoming of Wilson to his football team as the starting quarterback on June 27, 2011.

Before joining Wisconsin, Wilson had already earned a bachelor's degree in broadcast communications from North Carolina State. When he signed with the Badgers, he pursued a master's degree in educational leadership and policy analysis.

Wilson was able to sign with Wisconsin because he had a year of eligibility remaining. Under NCAA rules, an athlete can play a sport for four seasons. In Wilson's case, he redshirted as a freshman at North Carolina State. This meant his four-year eligibility as an NCAA athlete carried over into 2011, the year he became a Wisconsin Badger.

The fact that Wilson had an undergraduate degree also meant that the NCAA transfer rules did not apply to him. Under normal circumstances, a player must sit out an entire season if he or she transfers to another school. Not in Wilson's case. He was able to bring his arsenal of skills to Wisconsin without having to worry about a year-long layoff.

He made it known he wanted to sign with a national title contender. He reveals that around 30 teams reached out to him. He eventually whittled his choices down to just two teams: the Wisconsin Badgers and then-defending national champions Auburn Tigers. Between the two squads, Wisconsin had a bigger need for a top-tier quarterback.

Charlie McFall, Wilson's high school football coach at Collegiate School in Virginia, said Wisconsin was the team that did the most research on his former play caller. Wilson made such an immediate impact with the Badgers that they named him co-captain. Once he arrived on their campus, "Russellmania" became the norm.

His season with the Badgers increased his chances of playing in the NFL. In his first game, Wilson passed for 255 yards, rushed for 62 yards, had a 42-yard rushing touchdown, and completed 2 touchdown passes. They won that opening game against the UNLV Runnin' Rebels, 51-17. Wilson gave plenty of credit to his offensive line. "I don't think I got touched at all today," he told reporters after the game, "which is pretty unbelievable."

At the end of the regular season, Wilson it was named to the First Team of the All-Big Ten by both the coaches and the media that followed his career. The conference also named him its Griese-Brees Big Ten Quarterback of the Year. Wisconsin lost just two regular-season games.

The first loss occurred on the road against the 16th-ranked Michigan State Spartans on Oct. 22, 2011. The home team was up, 31-17, with just eight minutes left. However, sixth-ranked Wisconsin rallied. Wilson ran in for a touchdown and then threw a 2-yard touchdown pass to running back Montee Ball to tie the score. Spartans quarterback Kirk Cousins (now the starting quarterback for the Washington Redskins) threw a desperation 44-yard heave to wide receiver Keith Nichol with no time left. Officials initially said the ball did not cross the goal line, only to overturn the ruling minutes later. Final score: Michigan State 37, Wisconsin 31.

The next and last loss the Badgers suffered came at the hands of their conference foes, the Ohio State Buckeyes, exactly a week later. This, too, was another down-to-the-wire finish. Wisconsin was one of the nation's highest-scoring teams–it averaged 47.4 points and 512 all-purpose yards coming into the much-anticipated contest. Wilson continued to impress. He went 20-of-32 for 253 yards and 3 touchdown passes.

The game featured 4 touchdowns in the final four minutes and 39 seconds. Buckeyes freshman quarterback Braxton Miller started things off with a 44-yard scamper down the middle to give his team a 26-14 lead. The Badgers countered just 44 seconds later. Wilson connected with junior wide receiver Jared Abbrederis for a 17-yard touchdown to trim the deficit to 26-21 after the conversion.

Ohio State went three and out on the ensuing possession. Once the Badgers got the ball back, they needed just four plays to reach the end zone once again. Wilson found Jared Abbrederis by his lonesome on the left sideline and Abbrederis ran it in for a 49-yard touchdown. Wisconsin Coach Bret Bielema decided to go for the 2-point conversion. It succeeded, to make the score 29-26.

The Buckeyes managed to move the sticks to the Badgers' 40-yard line with just 30 seconds left. On first down, Miller eluded a Wisconsin blitz by rolling to his right. He spotted wide receiver Devin Smith all alone in the end zone. The freshman quarterback threw the ball to him. Touchdown. The sold-out crowd of 105,511 at Ohio Stadium erupted. Final score: Ohio State 33, Wisconsin 29.

Wilson led the Badgers to the 2012 Rose Bowl, one of the most prestigious college bowl games. During the Rose Bowl, Wilson had 19 pass completions for a total of 296 yards. He also had 18 rushing yards, he threw 2 touchdown passes, and he had 1 rushing touchdown. While Wilson showed himself as a tremendous quarterback throughout the Rose Bowl, the Badgers ended up falling short of winning the game, losing 45-38.

Wilson threw 33 touchdown pass, which set a Wisconsin season record. He also set the NCAA Football Bowl Subdivision record for highest pass completion percentage in a season. He completed an astonishing 72.8 percent of his passes. He threw just 4 interceptions all season long.

When asked how he felt about his one-year stint with the Badgers, Wilson said it exceeded his expectations. "Was it everything I expected?" he said. "Definitely everything I expected–and maybe a little more."

For his part, Bielema dubbed Wilson "a complete human being" after their one-year relationship ended.

College Baseball

Just like most of his family, Russell Wilson played dual sports in college. In addition to football, he played baseball for the North Carolina State University Wolfpack between 2008 and 2010. As mentioned earlier, Wilson was drafted by the Colorado Rockies and played for the Tri-City Dust Devils, which is a Class A Short Season team affiliated with the Colorado Rockies in the Northwest League.

During his college baseball career with the North Carolina Wolfpack, Wilson batted .282 in 2008, .384 in 2009, and .415 in 2010. He had 5 home runs and 30 runs batted in (RBIs). His ability to dramatically increase his batting average throughout his college career is what eventually made him a highly demanded baseball recruit for the Colorado Rockies in 2011. Wilson didn't play baseball for Wisconsin.

Elliott Avent is the North Carolina State Wolfpack baseball coach. He says his team would be roughly two-and-a-half months into the season when Wilson joined them. By then, there already had been starters in place at the second baseman and third baseman positions. Avent says it was tough to find a spot for Wilson in the infield rotation. As a result, he assigned Wilson to the outfield for the Wolfpack.

Avent's fondest memory of Wilson's baseball career at North Carolina State was when he hit a two-run, walk-off home run during a Coastal Carolina tournament game against the UC Irvine Anteaters. Wilson crushed the ball into a palm tree against a strong wind.

Just before Wilson signed with the Wisconsin Badgers, he played 61 games for the Asheville (N.C.) Tourists, the Class A South Atlantic League farm team of the Rockies. During that span, he batted .228 with three home runs, 15 runs batted in (RBIs), and 15 stolen bases.

Jay Matthews, scouting supervisor for the Colorado Rockies, says he first saw Wilson play baseball at the Commonwealth Games for high school students in Virginia. The Collegiate School standout was a relative unknown heading into the tournament. However, many came away impressed with his athleticism afterward. One of them was Matthews.

Not only was he raving about Wilson's athletic prowess, but he also singled out his leadership skills and learning abilities. He and his staff thought if Wilson could get enough exposure in their farm system (at least 1,000 at-bats), he would blossom as a baseball player. They believed he was tremendous on the defensive side of the ball. His offense would eventually improve as they developed his overall game.

Plus, Matthews says Wilson "had an average arm." Despite Wilson's flaws, the Rockies believed he was well worth the gamble.

Matthews compared the Rockies' new prospect to Jerry Hairston, the MLB veteran who suited up for nine teams during his 16-year stint in the majors. The Colorado scouting supervisor notes that both Wilson and Hairston had could play multiple positions on the field.

Joe Mikulik served as the Asheville Tourists' manager from 2000-2012. He also says Wilson struggled on offense.

What set him apart from the others was his raw talent and dedication. As a matter of fact, Mikulik says Wilson's work ethic "was by far the best we had on our squad." He would get up early and dedicate himself to baseball all day long. Wilson even practiced his hitting in the batting cage at noon when everyone else was at home.

Mikulik also loved Wilson's base-running instincts and athleticism in stealing bases. He also said Wilson improved at not getting tagged out when he reached base.

For his part, former Asheville Tourists outfielder Tyler Massey was taken aback when he first saw Wilson in spring training. "I was like, 'Wow, this guy's a Division I quarterback?' Because he was so short." He, too, swore by Wilson's work ethic. He said the latter would play six innings as a starter and do more extra work afterward, usually bunting 100 balls and taking another 100 to 200 swings. These were already in addition to the regular batting practices and drills the Tourists had.

Once Wilson's stint with the North Carolina Wolfpack was over, Mikulik said a lot of schools were calling his team inquiring about his availability for football. Wilson asked his manager for permission to go on several recruiting trips. He promised he would make it back.

Mikulik recalls it was around a week into the second half of the Tourists' season when Wilson informed him about his decision to commit to the Wisconsin Badgers' football program. Mikulik, Wilson, and general manager Larry Hawkins were in the clubhouse when this happened. The Tourists' manager encouraged his player to tell his teammates as well.

Mikulik described Wilson informing him of his major decision as "a pretty cool little moment."

2012 Senior Bowl

Expectations were riding high on Wilson as the 2012 Senior Bowl approached. It is a game held annually in Mobile, AL, featuring NFL prospects who have completed their college eligibility. Among his teammates were Michigan State quarterback Kirk Cousins, Nebraska Cornhuskers linebacker Lavonte David, and Boise State Broncos running back Doug Martin. Former Minnesota

Vikings head coach Leslie Frazier called the shots for the squad.

The moment Frazier met Wilson, he was impressed.

When Wilson flew into town, Frazier recalls him arriving on a Sunday night. One of the first things the highly-touted quarterback discussed was family: his and Frazier's. The head coach quickly fell in love with Wilson's assertiveness, reliability, and take-charge attitude. "Guys loved playing with him," Frazier said. "Observing him in the huddle, how he barked out the plays with command, how in control he was, spitting out information and doing it with authority. He was impressive." He named Wilson as the captain of the North team.

Frazier also lauded Wilson's preparation for the Senior Bowl. His knowledge of the offense suggested he had studied the playbook in advance. More proof of Wilson's football knowledge revealed itself in the film room–he discussed the plays with his coaches and teammates without trying too hard to make an impression. Frazier noted Wilson's humility is something "many players miss."

"Some guys are trying to make an impression so you can fall in love with them, but it's false," Frazier quips. "He wasn't trying to be something different than what he actually is–a leader."

Wilson went 4-of-7 passing, with a touchdown and an interception in the 2012 Senior Bowl. The North team prevailed over the South Team, 23-13.

Conclusion

Russell Wilson's success as an athlete in both his college football and baseball career led him to be highly in demand by both the National Football League and Major League Baseball. Wilson showed that he was not only a highly competitive athlete, but he also proved it by continuously improving his stats and performance. Ultimately, this is why he was recruited by the Colorado Rockies, as well as why the Seattle Seahawks drafted him.

Probably another outstanding characteristic was that Wilson was able to switch over to Wisconsin and start as a quarterback there after playing three seasons with North Carolina. He was able to show that he could quickly learn an entirely new offensive system and lead the team to a major bowl game. Most college quarterbacks would find this tough. For Wilson, it proved that he could start with a brand-new team and still be a successful starting quarterback.

While there are a lot more quarterbacks in college football who are shorter than the average height for a quarterback, Wilson also proved that he could still compete as a starting quarterback even though he is only 5-feet-11 inches tall. For a quarterback of his height to even be considered for the NFL, they have to not only demonstrate athletic ability but also prove themselves as being winning offensive leaders. Russell Wilson never looked at his height disadvantage as something that would get in his way, as he continuously worked toward showing the NFL that he was a well-deserving athlete who could play at that level.

Chapter 4: Russell's NFL Career

On January 16, 2012, Russell Wilson started training for the NFL Scouting Combine in Bradenton, Florida. The NFL Scouting Combine is a one-week event in which college football players perform both mental and physical tests to help coaches, general managers and other scouts to evaluate players for the draft. College players can attend the Scouting Combine by invitation only. It is vital for players to play at their best during the Scouting Combine because it not only determines whether a team drafts a player, but it can also determine the amount of salary they can negotiate.

Before the 2012 draft, scouts in the NFL projected that Russell Wilson would most likely be a middle-round pick. The primary reason that Wilson was not a number one draft pick was most likely his height. If he were 4 to 6 inches taller, it is very likely that he would have been a top draft pick. None other than Chris Weinke, a former NFL quarterback and currently the director of the IMG Madden Football Academy, and Jon Gruden, an ESPN analyst, said so.

The NFL's official website also cited Wilson's height as a possible impediment to his draft stock. More specifically, it said this "will be his biggest inhibitor at the next level." It also had some doubts about his ability to throw from the pocket. The website projected him to be a late first-round pick.

On the plus side, NFL.com lauded Wilson's passing accuracy. Despite its doubts about his pocket-passing abilities, it gave him props for his ability to evade pass rushers. The website also marveled at Wilson's athletic ability. It gave credit to him for being able to "torque his body to make any sort of throw on the run." Other pluses were his leadership and arm strength.

Wilson's 2012 NFL Scouting Combine results were: 4.55 seconds in the 40-yard dash, 34.0 inches in the vertical jump, 118.0 inches in the broad jump, 6.97 seconds in the three-cone drill, and 4.09 seconds in the 20-yard shuttle. He placed second in the 40-yard dash among quarterback aspirants. The Baylor Bears' Robert Griffin III (the Washington Redskins eventually drafted him second overall) came out on top with a time of 4.41 seconds. The

LSU Tigers' Jordan Jefferson (4.65 seconds) finished third while the Stanford Cardinal's Andrew Luck (4.67 seconds) finished fourth.

Once everything was said and done, NFL.com gave Wilson an overall grade of 68.5. Based on the website's criteria, he had a chance "to become Pro Bowl-caliber player."

The Draft

The Seattle Seahawks selected Russell Wilson in the third round of the 2012 NFL draft. He went 75th overall. Many criticized the Seahawks for their draft choices that year, especially the selection of Wilson. Again, their criticism was because he was only 5'11", which would make him one of the shortest quarterbacks in the NFL. On average, an NFL quarterback's height is around 6 feet 4 inches, meaning that Wilson is 5 inches shorter than most quarterbacks in the league.

Another reason for criticizing Russell Wilson was that the Seahawks had already signed a potentially good free-agent quarterback: Matt Flynn. Flynn had become a free agent after fulfilling his contract with the Green Bay Packers.

The Seahawks signed Flynn to a three-year, $20.5 million deal. This made him a substantially more expensive quarterback than Wilson, who was signed for only $2.9 million for four years. However, after the Seahawks had Flynn, Tarvaris Jackson (the starting quarterback for the Seahawks the previous season), and Wilson compete for the starting quarterback position, Wilson showed that he was the best choice to lead the team. Therefore, the Seahawks awarded Wilson the starting quarterback position for the 2012 season. They also dealt Jackson to the Buffalo Bills in exchange for a future draft pick to ease the logjam at quarterback.

Wilson quickly downplayed the doubts about his height and his overall game. "People tell me I'm too short," he said. "They've been telling me that my whole life. From my perspective, I think the main thing is I have all the other tools. I have big hands, long arms and I think the main thing is I have a big heart."

Wilson also assured Seahawks fans he could play at a very high level, given his track record as a starting quarterback in the ACC and Big Ten. He said the keys would be to compete to the best of his abilities and try to be efficient on every single play.

He also expressed his excitement about moving to Seattle, which he described as "a beautiful city." He told reporters in the aftermath of the draft he's aware of CenturyLink Field's reputation as a loud stadium. He said he couldn't wait to play in front of the Seahawks fans, one of the rowdiest fan bases in the NFL.

Wilson also told the media he was aware Flynn had just arrived in Seattle. He knew about the latter's reputation dating back to his days with the Green Bay Packers. Both quarterbacks played at the same time in the state of Wisconsin (Flynn for the Packers, Wilson for the Badgers). Wilson recalls meeting Flynn once. The new Seahawks rookie described the veteran as "a tremendous quarterback."

For his part, Seahawks head coach Pete Carroll lauded Wilson shortly after his team drafted him. He marveled at his new quarterback's athleticism and ability to do things other players have never done before. Throw in Wilson's character, and Carroll believed he had the makings of a great quarterback. The Seattle head coach also said having Wilson on board instantly makes them a better team.

Debut

In the preseason, Wilson played his first home game against the Tennessee Titans. On August 11, 2012, Wilson had his preseason debut as starting quarterback against the Kansas City Chiefs. Carroll decided to make him the Seahawks' starter the rest of the way, including the regular season.

Wilson concluded his first preseason with a 63.5 percent passing rate, 5 touchdowns, and 1 interception. He added 150 rushing yards and 1 rushing touchdown.

On September 9, 2012, that Wilson made his regular-season debut against the Arizona Cardinals. The Seahawks lost the game, 20-16. Wilson completed 18 of 34 attempts, giving him a 53% passing completion rate, with 153 yards and 1 touchdown pass. He was greatly criticized for his performance, as he threw three consecutive incompletions at the Cardinals' 4-yard line in the waning moments of the game. His counterpart, Arizona quarterback Kevin Kolb, completed the decisive touchdown pass to wide receiver Andre Roberts with 4:59 left to play.

To top it all off, referee Bob Hermansen made a crucial mistake with 30 seconds left. At that point, the Seahawks called a timeout when it seemed they had none anymore. The critical moment came minutes earlier when a Seahawks player checked out of the game. Seattle should have lost one timeout. However, Hermansen announced to the crowd at the University of Phoenix Stadium that the clock stopped on that play. Therefore, the officials did not charge Seattle with a timeout. Hermansen admitted to his error once the game ended. He told the media "the clock had no bearing on the play at all" and that his crew should not have given the additional timeout to Seattle.

While his regular-season debut was not impressive, the Seahawks decided to keep Russell Wilson as their starting quarterback, and he continued to improve throughout the 2012 season.

The Remaining 2012 Regular and Post Season

After that opening loss, Russell Wilson began to become more comfortable in his position, and he helped the team win their next four games, giving them a 4-1 record. They ended the season with an 11-5 record, winning all of their games at home. Wilson finished his rookie season with 3,118 passing yards, 26 touchdown passes, 10 interceptions, and 3 fumbles for a passer rating of 100.0. He added 499 rushing yards and 4 rushing touchdowns for good measure.

During Wilson's first NFL season, the Seahawks shone brightly defensively–they allowed just 245 points to their opponents. They also allowed an average of just 306.2 yards per game, fourth lowest in the NFL. Among the stalwarts was defensive end Chris Clemons, who had 11.5 sacks. Seattle middle linebacker Bobby Wagner had 140 tackles while cornerback Richard Sherman had 8 interceptions. It was arguably the best defense in the entire league, thanks mainly to coordinator Gus Bradley.

Seattle entered the playoffs as the No. 5 seed in the Wild Card round. During the wildcard playoff round, The Seahawks played against the Washington Redskins. It was

Russell Wilson vs. Robert Griffin III, the highly-touted quarterback whom the Redskins drafted 73 places ahead of him. Griffin entered the game hobbling. He had sprained the lateral collateral ligament in his right knee during a game against the Baltimore Ravens several weeks earlier. He wore a brace during the game against Seattle.

Washington jumped to an early 14-0 lead after the first quarter. The Redskins amassed 129 yards during that span but were able to muster just 74 yards the rest of the way. Griffin accounted for 68 yards and 2 touchdowns during the game's first 15 minutes.

After a Steven Hauschka field goal put the Seahawks on the board, Wilson inched his team closer several plays later. He threw a 4-yard touchdown pass to fullback Michael Robinson to make it 14-10 in favor of Washington after the PAT. Hauschka struck again with a 29-yarder later on to trim the deficit to just one point at the half.

The third quarter was a defensive struggle with neither team able to score. Finally, Wilson led the charge in the fourth quarter. After he had engineered several first downs, running back Marshawn Lynch scored on a 27-yard touchdown run to give Seattle the lead for good. Seattle was successful on a two-point conversion to make it 21-14.

Two plays later, Griffin re-injured his knee as it bent the wrong way on second down. The intense pain prevented him from playing further. The Redskins' No. 2 quarterback, Kirk Cousins, took over for Griffin but couldn't overcome the deficit. Hauschka nailed his third field goal of the night to put the game out of reach. Final score: Seattle Seahawks 24, Washington Redskins 14.

Wilson went 15-of-26 passing for 187 yards and a touchdown. He added 67 yards on the ground. The win was the Seahawks' sixth in a row, dating back to the regular season. The victory also meant Wilson was the last remaining rookie quarterback in the playoffs. The same weekend that Griffin's Redskins lost to Wilson's Seahawks, Andrew Luck's Indianapolis Colts lost on the road in a Wild Card matchup against the Baltimore Ravens. The final score was 24-9.

The Seahawks next faced the Atlanta Falcons in the NFC Divisional Round. Behind quarterback Matt Ryan, Atlanta seized control of the game. Ryan threw 3 touchdown passes–one each to tight end Tony Gonzalez, wide receiver Roddy White and running back Jason Snelling–to help the Falcons take a 27-7 lead entering the fourth quarter.

However, Wilson and the Seahawks were not about to go down without a fight.

He took matters into his hands with his team down by 20. First, he scored on a 1-yard touchdown run. Minutes later, he connected with Seahawks tight end Zach Miller on a 3-yard touchdown pass to make it 27-21 in favor of the Falcons. On Seattle's next drive, it took Wilson just three passes to move the ball 50 yards downfield. He eluded Falcons linebacker Sean Witherspoon before passing to running back Marshawn Lynch, who ran it all the way to Atlanta's 3-yard line. Lynch eventually scored on a 2-yard run with just 31 seconds left to give Seattle the lead for the first time, 28-27.

After Ryan threw a 29-yard pass to wide receiver Harry Douglas, Falcons head coach Mike Smith called timeout. Once play resumed, Ryan connected with Gonzalez for a 19-yard pickup. Smith called time again. He sent in kicker Matt Bryant to win it for the Falcons with a field goal. Bryant's kick sailed right through the uprights, sending Atlanta to the NFC championship game. Wilson and the Seahawks were going home. Final score: Atlanta Falcons 30, Seattle Seahawks 28.

Wilson had proved he was no ordinary rookie quarterback. Despite falling short against the Falcons, he completed 24 of 36 passes for 385 yards with 2 touchdowns and 1 interception. He even led Seattle in rushing for this game with 60 yards on the ground.

"We had high, high hopes for the rest of the season," Wilson told reporters. "When the game was over, I was very disappointed. But walking back into the tunnel, I got so excited about next year. The resilience we showed was unbelievable."

While critics were very pessimistic about the capability of Russell Wilson as a starting quarterback, all of these criticisms quickly evaporated after the 2012 season. Wilson proved that he deserved to be the team's starting quarterback, and the Seahawks were confident that they had made the right choice.

Once all was said and done, Russell Wilson became the fourth-best passer in the NFL. He even broke Ben Roethlisberger's rookie record, set in 2004. In addition, Wilson's 26 touchdown passes in the regular season tied Peyton Manning's record for most TD passes by a rookie quarterback.

Russell Wilson was awarded the Pepsi Rookie of the Week for his victory over the New York Jets, defeating them 28-7. He also received FedEx Player of the Week for his role in defeating the Chicago Bears, 23-17. And Wilson was named the NFL Offensive Rookie of the Month for December after having a 5-0 record for the month. At the end of the season, Wilson was awarded a $220,000 performance bonus by the NFL.

Wilson earned his biggest accolade of the season when the league named him 2012 NFL Rookie of the Year on February 2, 2013. He beat other high-profile first-year backs such as Andrew Luck, Robert Griffin III, Alfred Morris, and Doug Martin. The press release on NFL.com says Wilson gained an advantage by playing better as the season wore on. For instance, he ran for 3 touchdowns in a Week 15 win over the Buffalo Bills. He also threw 4 touchdown passes in a Week 16 victory over the Seahawks' fierce NFC West rivals, the San Francisco 49ers.

As mentioned earlier, he was the last rookie quarterback standing in the postseason. Wilson's stellar play in the NFC wild card game against the Washington Redskins and in the NFC Divisional Round against the Atlanta Falcons was also taken into account. To top it all off, he became a starter in his very first year in the league by beating out veterans Matt Flynn and Tarvaris Jackson. All in all, Wilson earned eight nominations as NFL.com Rookie of the Week during the 2012 season.

Seahawks head coach Pete Carroll couldn't have said it any better when asked about his sentiments when his quarterback took home the honor.

"He's been more impressive as he's grown more and been able to allow us to expand things," Carroll said. "And take on ideas and concepts and game plan more so than I would have thought. It's been pretty exciting."

2013 Regular Season

Even having an impressive season in 2012, Russell Wilson surpassed all the records he reached as a starting quarterback in the 2013 season. Wilson started the season by leading his team to a 4-0 record to start the regular season. It was the first time in the Seahawks' franchise history they went undefeated in their first four games. The Seahawks lost in the fifth week to the Indianapolis Colts.

However, after losing to the Colts, the Seahawks went on a seven-game winning streak. The Seahawks then suffered back-to-back losses, against the San Francisco 49ers and the Arizona Cardinals, both teams in their own division. Wilson finally suffered his first loss at home in the game against the Cardinals. Arizona won it on a Michael Floyd 31-yard touchdown reception with 2:13 left in the game. The final score was 17-10. Wilson didn't have a very good game: He went 11-of-27 passing for 108 yards with a touchdown and an interception. After Floyd scored, Cardinals linebacker Karlos Dansby intercepted a Wilson pass intended for wide receiver Doug Baldwin. The ball bounced off Baldwin's arm before Dansby picked it off to seal the outcome.

It was the first time Seattle lost at CenturyLink Field since Dec. 24, 2011–a run of 14 games. When this streak began, Wilson was still with the Wisconsin Badgers and Tarvaris Jackson was the Seahawks' starting quarterback.

Nonetheless, the Seahawks ended the season with a 13-3 record. Russell Wilson's second year as Seattle's starting quarterback resulted in the team's best record since the 2005 NFL season. This not only made the Seahawks the division winners, but it also made them the No. 1 seed for the NFC title.

For the second straight season, Seattle was dominant on defense. It allowed just 4,378 yards the entire season–the least in the entire league. The Carolina Panthers placed second in yards allowed, but they surrendered almost 500 yards more than the Seahawks did. Seattle also allowed just 273.6 yards per game. No other NFL team limited its opponent to fewer than 300 yards per contest. To put things in perspective, the Seahawks allowed their opponents to score an average of 14.4 points per game. The league average was 23.4 points, a difference of 9 points per game.

As for Wilson, his second-year totals were nearly identical to those during his rookie year: 3,357 passing yards, 26 touchdowns and 9 interceptions for a passer rating of 101.2. His passing yardage ranked 16th in the NFL, surpassing Alex Smith, Robert Griffin III, Colin Kaepernick, Jay Cutler, and Aaron Rodgers.

2013 Postseason and Super Bowl XLVIII

Most fans and critics were extremely impressed with Russell Wilson's role in helping the Seahawks enter the postseason in his first two seasons in the NFL. However, nothing impressed them more than what Wilson achieved next–he would lead Seattle's historic postseason tear. It was something few other quarterbacks would be able to pull off.

Wilson didn't get off to a very good start during the 2013 NFC Divisional Round Game against the sixth-seeded New Orleans Saints. As a matter of fact, his 103 passing yards represented a career worst at that point of his NFL tenure. His previous low was the 108 passing yards he produced in the Week 16 loss to the Cardinals.

However, what matters more is Seattle got the victory.

For this particular game, it was Seahawks running back Marshawn "Beast Mode" Lynch who willed his team to victory. He wound up with a franchise playoff record of 140 rushing yards and 2 touchdowns in the crucial 23-15 win over the Saints. His second touchdown was similar to the one he scored during the 2010 postseason–the one NFL fans remember as the "Beast Quake" touchdown run.

Despite Wilson struggling almost all game long, he connected on a 31-yard pass to wide receiver Doug Baldwin with 2:57 remaining. At this point, Seattle was up by a point, 16-15. On the very next play, Lynch cut to the outside and burst through the hole his teammates Zach Miller and Jermaine Kearse opened up for him. Lynch then stiff-armed New Orleans cornerback Keenan Lewis, the only defender remaining in his path, on his way to the end zone. The Seahawks were now up by 8 and CenturyLink Field was delirious.

The Seahawks' defense rose to the occasion yet again. It limited Saints tight end Jimmy Graham, the NFL's most prolific tight end, to just 1 reception for 8 receiving yards. Graham had finished the 2013 NFL season with 1,215 receiving yards. He was the only tight end to crack the league's Top 15 in this department. However, Seattle got the better of him on this day.

"We're not scared of him," Seahawks cornerback Richard Sherman had said before the game. "We have to deal with him, but he has to deal with us."

Wilson and his team next faced their bitter NFC West adversaries, Colin Kaepernick and the San Francisco 49ers, in the 2013 NFC title game.

It was the 49ers who jumped off to the early lead. They stymied the Seattle offense on their way to a 10-3 lead at the half. Kaepernick was unstoppable on the ground in the first two quarters. He gained 98 rushing yards during the game's first 30 minutes. He finished the game with 130 rushing yards.

Wilson made his presence felt in the waning moments of the first half. He threw a 51-yard pass to Doug Baldwin to set up a 32-yard field goal from Steven Hauschka to put Seattle on the board.

Behind a 40-yard touchdown scamper from Marshawn Lynch and a 40-yard field goal by Hauschka in the third quarter, Seattle stayed within striking distance, 17-13.

The Seahawks clamped down on defense in the final quarter, forcing the 49ers to commit three critical turnovers. Wilson and his teammates capitalized. On fourth down, he threw a 31-yard touchdown to wide receiver Jermaine Kearse in the opening moments of the fourth quarter. It was the first time Seattle tasted the lead.

San Francisco tried to regain the lead in the game's final moments. However, Richard Sherman tipped Kaepernick's pass, intended for wide receiver Michael Crabtree. Seattle linebacker Malcolm Smith caught the deflected pass to record the interception. Game over.

With this win, Wilson took his Seattle Seahawks to the Super Bowl in just his second season. Despite being sacked four times, he finished the game with 215 yards and 1 touchdown on 16-of-25 passing.

There was one obstacle left to overcome: Peyton Manning and the 2013 AFC Champions Denver Broncos.

Super Bowl XLVIII was set for February 3, 2014, at Giants Stadium in East Rutherford, N.J. On this day, Russell Wilson stood toe to toe with Manning to show that he was one of the league's best at his position.

In Wilson's first Super Bowl game, he went 18-of-25 passing for 206 yards and 2 touchdowns as his Seahawks cruised past Manning's Broncos, 43-8. Seattle was spectacular on all fronts—offense, defense and special teams—as it won its first-ever Vince Lombardi Trophy.

The Seahawks were already up 15-0 as the first half wound down when linebacker Malcolm Smith, the same player who intercepted Colin Kaepernick in the 2013 NFC Championship Game, recorded a pick-six off Manning to make it 22-0. Although Manning threw for 280 yards and 1 touchdown, he also threw 2 interceptions.

As the second half began, Percy Harvin padded the Seahawks' lead even more with a spectacular 87-yard kickoff return. His touchdown upped Seattle's lead to 29-0.

Wilson threw touchdown passes to Jermaine Kearse and Doug Baldwin in the latter stages of the game as the blowout was on. The Seahawks' quarterback recorded his NFL-record 29th victory after just two pro seasons. He was also the shortest quarterback and only the second African-American signal caller ever to win a Super Bowl. The first one was Doug Williams, who led the Washington Redskins to a 42-10 win over the Denver Broncos in Super Bowl XXII in 1988.

"We have been relentless all season," Wilson told the press afterward. "Having that mentality of having a championship day every day. At the end of the day, you want to play your best football, and that is what we did today."

As he finished his first season in the NFL, Wilson won many awards and was also awarded an estimated $169,000 from the NFL's performance-based program. However, it seems odd that he received a substantially lower bonus when he was able to assist his team in winning the Super Bowl. According to the Super Bowl XLVIII 2013 Postseason Media Guide, Wilson and his Seahawks teammates each received $92,000 for winning the game.

2014 Regular Season

The 2014 season began a whole new era for the Seahawks; for the first time in their NFL history they were the defending Super Bowl champions. For Russell Wilson, it was another season in which he would even further prove himself as one of the best quarterbacks in the NFL today.

In the Seahawks' third game of the regular season at CenturyLink Field on September 21, 2014, they played the Denver Broncos. The Broncos were out for revenge after having lost to Seattle in Super Bowl XLVIII. Wilson went 24-of-34 passing for 258 yards, 2 touchdowns, and 1 interception to lead Seattle to victory in overtime, 26-20. The Seahawks had a 17-3 lead in the fourth quarter but saw it dwindle after Peyton Manning engineered a late comeback to tie the score. However, Wilson completed 4 of 6 passes in the extra session and added 21 yards on the ground. After he had guided Seattle to the red zone on its first possession in overtime, running back Marshawn Lynch did the rest. He ran the ball in from 6 yards out to give the Seahawks the win. They were now 2-1 on the young season.

Several weeks after the win over Denver, Wilson continued to take his game to new heights. He set a new Monday Night Football record for a quarterback by rushing for 122 yards in a 27-17 road win over the Washington Redskins. He also completed 18 of 24 passes for 201 yards and two touchdowns. Wilson accounted for 323 all-purpose yards of the Seattle offense.

In this game, he played with the agility of a running back. He had runs of 16, 29, 13, and 22 yards in the game's first two drives alone. His outstanding performance helped propel Seattle to a 3-1 record. Once the final whistle blew, the Redskins were in awe of Wilson's performance.

"It was like he wasn't Superman in the second half," Washington safety Ryan Clark told the media. "He was, like, Clark Kent, half-Superman. He still did his thing."

Wilson was just getting started.

In Week 16, he completed 20 of 31 passes for a career-high 339 yards in a 35-6 blowout of the Arizona Cardinals on the road. Wilson threw both of his 2 touchdown passes to tight end Luke Willson. One of those was an 80-yard bomb. That was the longest pass the quarterback had ever thrown. Russell Wilson also ran for 55 yards on one play, establishing a new career best. He recorded 88 rushing yards for the game. The Seahawks set a new franchise record for most yards in a single game with 596. This despite the fact that the Cardinals had the third-best defense in the NFL. Both Seattle and Arizona were 11-4 at the conclusion of the game. The Seahawks snapped the Cardinals' seven-game win streak. More importantly, they clinched the top spot in the NFC West and the No. 1 seed in their conference for the second straight year. Seattle finished with a stellar 12-4 record to close out the 2014 regular season. The Seahawks now had to defend their crown with the luxury of hosting all their playoff games in the friendly confines of CenturyLink Field.

2014 Postseason and Super Bowl XLIX

The first team the Seahawks faced in the playoffs was the upstart Carolina Panthers. Even though the Panthers had finished just 7-8-1 in the regular season, they were the top team in the NFC South. Because of this, they had home-field advantage in the NFC wild card round against the Arizona Cardinals. Behind quarterback Cam Newton's 198 passing yards and 2 touchdowns, Carolina prevailed over Arizona, 27-16.

However, the Panthers proved to be no match for Wilson and Company.

Wilson started off the 2014 postseason on a high note. He passed for 268 yards and 3 touchdowns to lead the Seahawks to a 31-17 victory over the Panthers. He converted on all eight of his third-down attempts, frustrating the Carolina defense all game long. Those third-down conversions accounted for 199 yards of the Seattle offense. To top it all off, Wilson finished with a passer rating of 149.2. It was the second-highest of his brilliant career.

Wilson connected with wide receiver Doug Baldwin for a 16-yard touchdown in the first quarter. Late in the first half, he threw a 63-yard touchdown pass to Jermaine Kearse as Seattle held on to a 14-10 lead at halftime. With neither team scoring in the third quarter, Wilson took matters into his own hands. After a Steven Hauschka field goal, the Seahawks quarterback threw a 25-yard touchdown pass to tight end Luke Willson to give the home team a 24-10 lead.

The Panthers tried to rally. However, Newton couldn't find an open receiver as the Seattle secondary tightened up its defense. The Panthers' quarterback decided to pass the ball to tight end Ed Dickson. Seattle safety Kam Chancellor anticipated the move, stepped into the passing lane, intercepted the pass and took it the opposite way 90 yards for a defensive touchdown. It was Chancellor's third career pick-six. At that point, Seattle was up by 21 at 31-10. The Panthers couldn't recover, and the Seahawks were on their way to their second consecutive NFC Championship Game.

Up next for Wilson's crew were Aaron Rodgers and the Green Bay Packers. The latter had defeated the Dallas Cowboys at home, 26-21, to advance against Seattle. Down 21-13 with a little over four minutes left in the third quarter, the Packers rallied behind two Rodgers touchdowns. He connected with wide receiver Devante Adams for a 46-yard score late in the third quarter. He then threw a 13-yard touchdown pass to tight end Richard Rodgers in the fourth quarter.

In the NFC title game, it was Green Bay that seized control in the early going. After Mason Crosby made two first-quarter field goals, Rodgers threw a 13-yard touchdown pass to wide receiver Randall Cobb just as the quarter ended. Mason added another field goal in the second quarter to give Green Bay a 16-0 lead at halftime. Wilson threw 3 interceptions in the game's first 30 minutes. The fans at CenturyLink Field were stunned.

Surprisingly, it wasn't Wilson who put the Seahawks on the board. Punter Jon Ryan threw a 19-yard touchdown pass to tackle Garry Gilliam on a trick play to make it 16-7 in the third quarter. Crosby's field goal padded the Packers' lead to 19-7 with 10:53 left in the game. After six more minutes had elapsed on the game clock, Seattle hadn't scored again. Wilson threw his fourth interception of the game minutes later. The Seahawks then managed to orchestrate a seven-play, 69-yard drive, culminating in Wilson's 1-yard touchdown run to make it 19-14 with 2:09 remaining.

Seahawks head coach Pete Carroll decided to try the onside kick. Packers' tight end Brandon Bostick got a hand on the ball, but couldn't recover. Instead, Seattle's Chris Matthews secured possession for his team at the 50-yard line. Seahawks running back Marshawn Lynch scored on a 24-yard scamper to give his team the lead for the first time. Russell Wilson connected with Luke Willson for the two-point conversion to make it 22-19. CenturyLink Field was deafening.

However, the Packers still had time. Rodgers led a seven-play, 48-yard drive to put Green Bay within field-goal range. Crosby nailed his fifth field goal of the night to tie things up at 22 apiece.

In the overtime period, Wilson proved once again why he's one of the NFL's best quarterbacks. After the Seahawks won the coin toss, it took them just six plays to march the ball 87 yards downfield. Wilson threw a 35-yard touchdown pass to Jermaine Kearse with 3:19 gone by in the extra session. The home crowd exploded. The Seahawks were going to the Super Bowl for the second consecutive year.

Wilson was overjoyed. He was sobbing on the field after the hard-fought win over Green Bay. He gave credit to his teammates for never giving up.

"The will and the drive of these men is unbelievable," Wilson said. "We always find a way to finish…I'm honored to be on his team. I'm going to the Super Bowl again."

Despite making it to the Super Bowl again, the Seattle Seahawks needed to be at the top of their game. The reason? Waiting for them were Tom Brady and the three-time Super Bowl champions New England Patriots.

Super Bowl XLIX was set for February 2, 2015, at the University of Phoenix Stadium in Glendale, Ariz. The game lived up to the hype–it went down the wire to the very last possession.

Just as in the 2014 NFC Championship Game against the Green Bay Packers, Russell Wilson got off to a slow start. He was not able to connect with any of his receivers in the first quarter. Instead, it was Brady who struck first. He recorded his 50th career playoff touchdown pass in the first quarter when he threw to wide receiver Brandon LaFell for an 11-yard score. The Patriots led, 7-0.

Chris Matthews, the same player who recovered the critical onside kick in the NFC title game against the Packers, came up big for the Seahawks yet again. He caught a 44-yard pass from Wilson in the last few minutes of the second quarter. That was his first career catch. That set the stage for Seattle running back Marshawn Lynch. He galloped 3 yards into the end zone with 4:51 left in the first half to put his team on the board. His touchdown capped off an eight-play, 70-yard drive.

However, it didn't take long for New England to retaliate.

The Patriots have always been dangerous when it comes to their no-huddle schemes. Today was no exception. Brady orchestrated an eight-play, 80-yard drive of his own to set up a 22-yard bomb to tight end Rob Gronkowski with 31 seconds left in the first half. The Patriots led, 14-7.

But Wilson, who had got the better of Peyton Manning a year earlier, was not to be outdone. All it took for him to march the football 80 yards in five plays was a measly 29 seconds. That was almost two minutes faster than Brady just a series earlier. The crucial moment came when Seahawks wide receiver Ricardo Lockette caught a pass from Wilson. At the same time, Patriots cornerback Kyle Arrington was penalized for grabbing Lockette's facemask. The penalty was worth 15 yards, a substantial gain with the clock winding down. Seattle was then at New England's

10-yard line with six seconds left in the second quarter. Wilson promptly took advantage of Arrington's blunder. He lofted a pass to the left corner of the end zone for Chris Matthews. Touchdown. Seattle 14, New England 14.

After Katy Perry's Pepsi Super Bowl XLIX halftime show, it seemed Wilson and the Seahawks were on the verge of repeating.

Steven Hauschka's field goal made it 17-14 in favor of Seattle and Wilson then led a six-play, 50-yard drive with 4:51 remaining in the third quarter. That resulted in a Doug Baldwin touchdown to make it 24-14.

Unfortunately, it wasn't meant to be for the Seahawks.

Two-time Super Bowl MVP Tom Brady came through in the clutch for the Patriots. Two of his four touchdown passes came in the fourth quarter–one to Danny Amendola and the other to Julian Edelman. The second touchdown proved to be the dagger as New England took the lead, 28-24.

With time down to 2:02, the Seahawks still had a chance to win the game. With 1:06 left, Wilson let go of a 33-yard heave that wide receiver Jermaine Kearse caught in spectacular fashion at New England's 5-yard line. Lynch rushed for a 4-yard gain. This set up second-and-goal at the Patriots' 1-yard line.

And then it happened.

Wilson threw toward Lockette on a slant route headed into the end zone. As Lockette was about to make the catch, Patriots rookie cornerback Malcolm Butler stepped into the passing lane. He knocked Lockette to the turf as he intercepted Wilson's pass. Game over.

Final score: New England Patriots 28, Seattle Seahawks 24.

The Patriots won their fourth Vince Lombardi Trophy in the Tom Brady and Bill Belichick era. Brady also won his third Super Bowl MVP. It was especially sweet for Patriots fans, who had waited 10 years to win another title.

Many experts criticized the Seahawks for calling that receiving play, especially with a running back of Lynch's caliber around. When reporters asked Wilson about the Butler interception, he said he thought it was a touchdown.

"I thought it was a touchdown, honestly," Wilson said. "Unfortunate situation, man. We played lights out for the most part. We fought so hard. You've got to give the Patriots credit. Tom made some great plays out there, and he was clutch at the end of the game."

He also didn't deny the fact this loss hurts.

"It definitely hurts," Wilson said. "You think about everything you go through all year and all the ups and downs, just how great we played throughout this game. At the same time, I love the guys that I have around me, I love the people I have around me, so I hate feeling I'm the one who lost it, in a way. For me, I keep my head up, though."

Despite the loss, the Seahawks have experienced the most success they have ever had since their inaugural season in 1974. It remarkably all occurred right after Russell Wilson became their quarterback.

2015 Regular Season

Before Russell Wilson's fourth season even began, he reaped the benefits of the hard work he had put in.

On July 31, 2015, the Seattle Seahawks signed Wilson to a lucrative four-year extension worth $87.6 million, with $60 million in guaranteed money. The deal also included a $31 million signing bonus, the highest ever in Seahawks franchise history. The previous high was $12 million for wide receiver Percy Harvin (now with the Buffalo Bills). The new contract also made Wilson, an unheralded third-round draft pick three years ago, the second-highest paid NFL player. Wilson's agent, Mark Rodgers, and Seahawks General Manager John Schneider negotiated for four days. They finally struck a deal at 11 p.m. on July 31.

Wilson's base salaries are: $700,000 in 2015, $12.34 million in 2016, $12.6 million in 2017, $15.5 million in 2018, and $17 million in 2019.

Wilson said he was always optimistic he would get a better deal with the Seahawks.

"I was excited about it, you know. I'm always an optimist, an ultimate one. I was always believing that it would work out."

While Wilson got his hefty paycheck, he didn't start the 2015 NFL season as he hoped he would.

He threw 10 touchdown passes and 7 interceptions in the Seahawks' first nine games. Because Wilson was not at his best, neither was Seattle. During that span, the team sported a below average 4-5 (.444) win-loss record. As a matter of fact, the Seahawks lost their first two games of the season. They lost to the St. Louis Rams, 34-31, in Week 1. The following week, they lost, 27-17, to the Green Bay Packers.

However, Wilson flipped the switch somehow.

All of a sudden, he found his touch beginning in Week 11. That was when the Seahawks beat the San Francisco 49ers, 29-13. In that game, Wilson completed an astonishing 24 of 29 passes for 260 yards, 3 touchdowns, and no interceptions.

Wilson had his best game of the season, and perhaps the best regular-season game of his young career, on his 27th birthday. It happened in a Week 12 game against the visiting Pittsburgh Steelers. He threw a career-high 5 touchdown passes in the 39-30 victory. Two of those went to wide receiver Doug Baldwin in the game's final eight minutes. Wilson connected with Baldwin on an 80-yard score just before the two-minute warning. It occurred after the Steelers had trimmed the 9-point deficit to 2 at 32-30. The Seahawks sported a 6-5 record after beating Pittsburgh. In all of Seattle's five losses, the team led in the fourth quarter but lost. Not this time. Two fourth-quarter interceptions courtesy of Richard Sherman and Kam Chancellor helped the Seattle cause.

As for Wilson, he could not have seen this big day coming.

He wasn't feeling very well on his birthday. He woke up at the team hotel feeling sick. He needed three intravenous (IV) feeds to play against Pittsburgh.

Despite Wilson's illness, he still recorded a 147.9 passer rating. It was his best in the 2015 NFL season. He came through in the clutch once again, going 7 of 9 for 164 yards and three touchdowns in the final quarter. For the game, Wilson was 21 of 30 passing for 345 yards and no interceptions. More importantly, it was the first time the

Seahawks went over the. 500 mark in the season. It proved to be a critical win in more ways than imaginable.

"That was a lot of fun," Wilson said. "It can't get any more fun."

What wasn't funny was the Seahawks losing prize tight end acquisition Jimmy Graham for the season. Graham landed in awkward fashion after he tried to catch a Wilson pass early in the fourth quarter. Trainers put a cast on his right leg and then carted him off the CenturyLink Field turf. The diagnosis: a patellar tendon injury.

Nonetheless, Wilson duplicated his stellar feat two weeks later.

Feeling much better this time, he threw 5 touchdown passes in a 35-6 demolition of the Baltimore Ravens at home. Once again, Wilson and Doug Baldwin were at the top of their game. The duo accounted for 3 touchdowns. Wilson had thrown 16 touchdown passes in the Seahawks' last four games, all of them wins. For this game, Wilson connected on 23 of 32 passes for 292 yards and, once again, no interceptions. Seattle held a 14-6 lead at the half but pulled away for good in the third and fourth quarters. During that span, the Wilson and Baldwin tandem scored two touchdowns. Wilson added a 49-yard touchdown pass to Tyler Lockett in the fourth quarter for good measure.

The Seahawks were peaking at the right time. They had won six of their last seven games to improve to 8-5 on the season and they were inching closer to an NFC wild card spot.

Since the Week 10 win over the 49ers, Wilson had been on fire. In a seven-game span to close out the 2015 NFL season, he threw 24 touchdowns with just 1 interception. Seattle went 6-1 during that stretch. As Wilson went, so did the Seahawks.

Wilson's fourth season proved that he belonged in the upper echelon of NFL quarterbacks. He had a passer rating of 110.1. His completion percentage (68.3), accuracy (78.4), deep passing accuracy (49.2), and accuracy under pressure (71.6) were all good for third among NFL quarterbacks. He also helped Seattle gain an average of 8.3

yards every time he completed a pass. That was fourth among all NFL signal callers.

Wilson shone brightest in the face of adversity. He played better when the Seahawks were staring playoff elimination in the face. He also took his play to the next level when Seattle missed several key players.

Wilson recorded an amazing passer rating of 132.8 from Weeks 11 to 17. During this stretch, the team was without tight end Jimmy Graham and running back Thomas Rawls. They also lost star running back Marshawn Lynch for a few games. At that point in the season, the Seahawks were just 5-5.

Wilson also proved to be very efficient at moving the football at critical junctures. Proof of this was his 79.0 completion rate on third downs since Week 11. That was the best among NFL quarterbacks. It was quite an improvement from his 56.5 completion rate through the first 10 weeks of the season.

His chemistry with wide receiver Doug Baldwin was fantastic. He completed an astonishing 80.4 percent of his throws to the wide receiver. That was the highest figure of any quarterback/wide receiver tandem in the last 10 years. In the last seven weeks of the 2015 NFL season, Wilson connected on 47 of his 59 passes to Baldwin. That translated to a 150.3 passer rating. Baldwin wasn't too shabby himself–he amassed 78 catches for 1,069 yards and 14 touchdowns on the season. It tied him with the New York Jets' Brandon Marshall, the Jacksonville Jaguars' Allen Robinson, and the Atlanta Falcons' Devonta Freeman for most touchdown receptions in the league.

For his part, Wilson wasn't done.

He set several franchise records during his breakout 2015 NFL campaign. He established a new team record for passing yards in a season with 4,024. He remains the only Seattle Seahawks quarterback ever to surpass the 4,000-yard mark in a season. Matt Hasselbeck previously held the franchise record with 3,966 passing yards, a feat he achieved in 2007.

Wilson also became the Seahawks' all-time leader for most touchdown passes in a single season with 34 in 2015. That was two better than Dave Krieg's previous record of 32 touchdown passes in 1984.

Finally, Wilson became the first NFL player to amass at least 4,000 passing yards, 30 touchdown passes, and 500 rushing yards in a single season. In just his fourth NFL season, Russell Wilson was already breaking all sorts of NFL records. At just 27 years old, it's a safe bet he will break some more in the next few years.

2015 Postseason

The Seahawks faltered to a poor 4-5 start to the 2015 NFL season. However, they were able to regroup and finish with a 10-6 record mainly due to Russell Wilson's heroics. Seattle secured an NFC wild card spot against 2012 NFL MVP Adrian Peterson and the Minnesota Vikings.

The game took place on January 10, 2016, at the University of Minnesota's TCB Bank Stadium. On this day, luck would prove to be the difference. The Seahawks, just as in the 2014 NFC Championship Game against the Green Bay Packers, got off to a slow start.

Three Blair Walsh field goals put the Vikings in front, 9-0, through the first three quarters. The Seahawks had a golden opportunity to score in the second quarter. Wilson spotted a wide open Doug Baldwin in the end zone. However, the Minnesota secondary batted the ball down. Wilson and his team had another chance in the third quarter when backup tight end Chase Coffman made his way to the end zone. However, Wilson overthrew the pass, and the ball bounced off Coffman's fingertips. Vikings cornerback Trae Waynes intercepted it. Seattle, with a previously red-hot Russell Wilson, had yet to score in a pivotal playoff game.

That was, until the amazing Russell Wilson-Doug Baldwin tandem came through for the Seahawks again.

Wilson orchestrated a seven-play, 80-yard drive in the early minutes of the fourth quarter. It culminated in his 3-yard touchdown pass to Baldwin with 11:37 remaining in the game. Minnesota still held a precarious two-point lead at 9-7.

Unfortunately for the Vikings, they just could not hang on. Adrian Peterson fumbled on the next series and the

Seahawks recovered. Three minutes later, Seattle had moved the sticks 12 yards but could not go any further. They went for the 46-yard field goal try on fourth down. Steven Hauschka made it to give the Seahawks the lead for the first time at 10-9.

With 1:42 left, the Vikings had the ball on their own 39-yard line. They somehow put themselves in a position to re-take the lead. One big factor was a pass interference penalty on Seattle safety Kam Chancellor.

It eventually set the stage for Walsh.

Minnesota milked the clock down to just 22 seconds to set up a game-winning field goal try. It was a 27-yard attempt. Walsh had already made three field goals, including two from 43 and 47 yards out. There was no reason for him to miss this one.

He missed.

For some reason, Walsh's attempt sailed wide left. It wasn't even anywhere near the left upright. The Seahawks had pulled off a stunner, 10-9.

Wilson just played a mediocre game–he went 13-of-26 passing with one touchdown and one interception. The Vikings also sacked him twice. Despite Wilson's average stat line, the Seahawks moved on to face the resurgent Carolina Panthers in the NFC Divisional Round.

The Seahawks took on the Panthers at the latter's Bank of America Stadium in Charlotte, N.C., on Jan. 18, 2016. It was a highly anticipated matchup between two of the league's best young quarterbacks–Seattle's Russell Wilson and Carolina's Cam Newton.

As had been the trend in the Seahawks' most recent postseason games, they played from behind once again. The Seahawks were the second-best defensive team in 2015, allowing just 291.8 yards per game. Seattle and the Denver Broncos were the only two squads that allowed fewer than 300 yards per contest. On the other hand, the Panthers were no pushovers on defense, either. With stalwarts such as middle linebacker Luke Kuechly and cornerback Josh Norman in the fray, Carolina was a dangerous team. The Panthers were sixth in the NFL in fewest yards allowed per game (322.9). They made life hard for Wilson in the 2015 NFC Divisional Round.

Carolina got on the board first. Running back Jonathan Stewart started things off with a 59-yard scamper on the Panthers' opening drive. That gave Carolina good field position. Three plays later, Stewart ran the ball into the end zone from 4 yards out for a 7-0 lead. He had just come back from a foot injury.

Wilson didn't get off to a very good start in this one. Seattle had possession with less than 12 minutes to go in the first quarter. On second and 13 from the Seahawks' own 11-yard line, he took the snap from center Patrick Lewis. Panthers defensive tackle Kawann Short pursued Wilson, who overthrew a pass intended for running back Marshawn Lynch. The ball fell right into the waiting arms of Kuechly, who took it the other way for the pick-six. Carolina was up, 14-0, after 15 minutes of play.

The Panthers did not relent in the second quarter. Stewart struck again with another touchdown run – a short, 1-yard leap – for a 21-0 lead after the PAT with just 42 seconds gone by in the period. On the Seahawks' ensuing drive, the Panthers stifled Wilson yet again. This time, Carolina cornerback Cortland Finnegan intercepted Wilson at Seattle's 29-yard line. Graham Gano then made a 48-yard field goal to put the Panthers ahead, 24-0.

Six minutes later, Newton threw the ball to tight end Greg Olsen in double coverage in the end zone. The fact the Seahawks' second-best defense bottled up Olsen didn't matter. He hauled it in for a touchdown to make it a commanding 31-0 lead for the Panthers.

In spite of the huge deficit, the Seahawks did not wilt under pressure in the second half. In fact, they put up a gallant stand.

Seattle took the ball to the air to get its offense going in the second half. Wilson threw touchdown passes to Jermaine Kearse and Tyler Lockett in the third quarter to make it 31-14. With six minutes remaining in the fourth quarter, Wilson found Kearse in the end zone for the second time. Kearse scored on a 3-yard reception with All-Pro cornerback Josh Norman covering him. The Seahawks still had a pulse. It was now 31-21 in favor of Carolina.

Wilson drove the Seahawks 60 yards on 11 plays late in the fourth quarter. Steven Hauschka made a 36-yard field goal. Seattle inched closer. Wilson and his team were now down by just a touchdown. However, time was not on their side, as there was only 1:12 left to play.

Head coach Pete Carroll decided to go for the onside kick. The Seahawks hoped they would be as lucky they were almost a year ago when they recovered an onside kick against the Green Bay Packers in the 2014 NFC Championship Game.

It wasn't meant to be.

Panthers linebacker Thomas Davis recovered Hauschka's onside kick. Newton took a knee to end matters. The Carolina Panthers were going to Super Bowl 50 to face Peyton Manning's Denver Broncos. The Seattle Seahawks were going home.

Wilson's stat line: 31-of-48 passing for 366 yards, 3 touchdowns and 2 interceptions. The Panthers sacked him five times. His two-year run of guiding his Seattle Seahawks to the Super Bowl had come to an end.

Despite the loss, Wilson gave his team credit for the second-half comeback.

"In the second half, we had to go for it," Wilson said. "We had to come out swinging. That was our mentality, and we did a great job of that."

Wilson's season may not have ended the way he wanted it. Nonetheless, he registered what was his best statistical season to date. The trend for the 2015 NFL season was his ability to come through in the face of adversity. His numbers and his relentlessness are the reasons why he is now considered one of the NFL's elite quarterbacks.

Russell's Height

There are many requirements that the NFL has for a quarterback, and the one that Russell Wilson lacks is height. He is only 5'11", and the average quarterback is around 6'4". Many football experts believe height is an important trait in quarterbacks because they need to have a good view down the field, as well as being able to keep the defense from stuffing their throws.

Russell Wilson was a third-round draft pick in 2012. Yes, his athleticism and leadership abilities in college were extremely impressive. Despite this, Wilson was not drafted until the third round. But why? Probably because many did not consider him a first-round draft pick due to his height.

While Russell Wilson had above-average stats during his college career as a quarterback, many scouts did not consider them relevant, especially when it came to playing in the NFL, because it is a completely different beast to compete in the most competitive American football league in the world.

And now, fast forward to today: Russell Wilson is the league's shortest starting quarterback, with Drew Brees right just above him at 6-foot even. In fact, Brees was one of Wilson's role models who provided him with the motivation and encouragement that he could also competitively play as a quarterback in the NFL. Brees had the most passing yards in one season in 2011, but his record was broken by one yard by Peyton Manning in 2013. Brees also has the most seasons (four) with more than 5,000 passing yards. No other quarterback has had more than one season with over 5,000 yards passing.

And, while Russell Wilson has not come close to passing over 5,000 yards in a single season, he is still showing the world that he belongs in the NFL. He has back-to-back Super Bowl appearances in his second and third seasons as a starting quarterback, as well as winning the Super Bowl in the 2013 season.

So when you look at players like Russell Wilson, and even Drew Brees, does height really matter? Well, Russell Wilson shows that it should not be a determining factor. He has athleticism, he has leadership skills, he has intelligence, and probably most important, he has heart. All of these other factors more than make up for his height disadvantage.

Wilson has downplayed skeptics' remarks about his height. After all, he has had to deal with these people since his college days at North Carolina State and Wisconsin.

Perhaps winning a Super Bowl title will make them think twice about criticizing him again.

Wilson made this point in the aftermath of the 43-8 win over the Denver Broncos in Super Bowl XLVIII. He said his leadership abilities and relentlessness are the qualities that make him excel at the game's highest level.

"God's given me so much talent and my height doesn't define my skill set," Wilson said. "I believe that God has given me a right arm and for some reason even though I'm 5'11" to be able to make the throws and make great decisions on the field and all that.

"I think to be a great quarterback, you have to have great leadership, great attention to detail, and a relentless competitive nature," Wilson emphasized. "And that's what I try to bring to the table and I have a long way to go. I'm still learning and I'm still on a constant quest for knowledge."

The Seahawks were truly fortunate to have Russell Wilson lead their team. In fact, he could easily be traded today to other teams that ended up choosing other first-round quarterbacks in 2012. So maybe height should not be a major consideration after all? Well, that is how Russell Wilson feels about it.

Conclusion

Playing for only four seasons in the NFL, Russell Wilson has already broken rookie records, led his team to four consecutive playoff seasons and two back-to-back Super Bowl championships, and ended up winning the 2013 season Super Bowl. No doubt, Russell Wilson will most likely be inducted into the Pro Football Hall of Fame, and he has only started his career as a professional NFL quarterback.

Chapter 5: Russell Wilson as a Leader

Many characteristics are required to be a great quarterback. The quarterback position is unique as it requires great leadership. While having leadership skills is extremely helpful, most football positions do not demand as many leadership skills as a starting quarterback, especially an NFL quarterback. For a quarterback, having leadership skills is an absolute must.

The quarterback is the person who receives the snap from center. Therefore, he must instantly take charge of the offense and read the defense to determine holes they can exploit. For instance, a quarterback must be able to determine quickly when the defense is attempting a rush, and quickly make adjustments. While he works directly with his coaches to come up with plays and how to work against their opponent's defense, it is up to the quarterback himself to communicate with his teammates and get them 100% committed to making a play on every down. This does not simply call for athletic ability, but it also requires the quarterback to have a charisma that inspires the entire team.

It is also vital for a quarterback to be able to help his team make quick adjustments when things go wrong. It is a trait necessary whether the quarterback himself made the mistake, or one of the other offensive line players fails to do his part. The quarterback must have a short-term memory, meaning he must quickly forget about what recently happened, let the past be the past, and motivate the offensive line to make the next big play.

For Russell Wilson, this is probably one of his greatest abilities on the field. He knows how to lead his team and get the job done. When he is on the field, you can see that he remains calm throughout the entire game. This calm composure spreads to the whole team. He also shows himself to be extremely confident and competitive. Many players on the Seattle Seahawks claim that Russell Wilson is one of the most successful quarterbacks because he is the most competitive player on the team. He loves winning, and he will do everything he possibly can to accomplish it. Again, this competitive spirit also transfers to his teammates, which is why they have been so successful since he has been their starting quarterback.

A Leader on and off the Field

Russell Wilson is not simply a leader on the field; he also presents a great example for his teammates and fans when he is not throwing the ball. For one thing, he holds strong Christian values. People notice this every time he attends a press conference or conducts an interview. Many would argue that his strong Christian values are among his greatest strengths as a leader, and Wilson himself would agree with this. He always manages to set a moral and ethical example to everyone around him. Ever since he has been with the Seattle Seahawks, Wilson has provided community service at a local children's hospital. He is very adamant about committing his time to children's hospitals, as he has been doing consistently doing every Tuesday since he started playing professionally.

Russell Always Prepares

A leading quarterback does not simply have an uncanny athletic ability, but he strives to be better than all of his teammates. And this is not just physically but, more important, mentally. Russell Wilson believes in the saying, "Separation is preparation." When he is not on the playing field or in training, he is consistently learning the plays, helping others understand the plays, and consistently studying tapes. He wants to learn what the best players are doing and how he can incorporate that into his game plan. He spends an ample amount of time with his coaches, ensuring he can receive all the knowledge they can bestow upon him. Before he plays against his next opponent, you will find Russell studying their defense so he can determine how to "crack their code."

This vital discipline from Wilson helps establish his role as a leader with the Seahawks in many ways. For one, it sets an example to the entire team that to become an all-time great player everyone should take time and prepare himself as much as possible. Additionally, it makes him the "go-to" guy for practically every player (both offense and defense). His knowledge of the game gives his entire team confidence that their quarterback knows how to make the big play—and that builds up the entire team's confidence that their quarterback is going to do everything he can to help them win the game.

NFC Championship Against the Green Bay Packers

The time when a quarterback really shows that he knows how to lead his team is when he brings them back to win from a large deficit. When the Seattle Seahawks played the NFC championship game against the Packers after the 2014 NFL season, many considered their comeback from a 19-7 deficit with only three minutes remaining as mere luck. It can be true that a little luck plays into any major rally, but there is no doubt that strong leadership skills and having a heart that says you can still win in such a situation are also required.

Trailing by 12 points and only having three minutes remaining, Wilson stunned the NFL world by taking his team to overtime to defeat the Packers and gain entry into the Super Bowl. Coaches and teammates never had a single bit of doubt in Wilson, as he remained confident and calm. He knew what he had to do. He knew that if he lost to the Packers, they would not be able to compete in the Super Bowl for a second consecutive season. He kept his team completely optimistic, and his positivity radiated to everyone around him.

Wilson's head coach, Pete Carroll, marveled at his competitive mindset after the come-from-behind win against the Packers.

"I think he's very, very special," Carroll quipped. "I don't know how he could play at the level that he plays, in the most challenging of times, with a tremendous mind. He's got a tremendous competitive mindset and it stems from the confidence that he feels based on the preparation that he puts in, knowing that he's ready for whatever comes up."

"You saw a tremendous illustration of that (against Green Bay)," Carroll added. "I don't think you could hope an athlete at this level could have a more clear mindset of what it takes to come through and get it done more so that what Russell has."

Jermaine Kearse, the Seahawks wide receiver who caught Wilson's game-winning pass against the Packers, is also in awe of his quarterback's leadership abilities.

"His leadership on the sideline, continuing to keep guys in it, was huge," Kearse said. "His power of positivity is huge. When you can stay competitive in situations like that, it's kind of hard to just crumble. That just shows the type of leader he is and the type of belief that he has in his teammates and in this team."

Just imagine, Russell Wilson was a third-round draft pick quarterback who was given very little chance of starting, mainly because of his height. Nevertheless, he has already made it to the Super Bowl twice and won it in his first appearance. Nobody will doubt his ability now, as he shows himself to be a great all-time NFL quarterback leader.

Seattle cornerback Richard Sherman expressed his thoughts on why Wilson's draft stock plummeted in 2012. Sherman made the comments after the win over Green Bay in the 2014 NFC Championship Game.

"It wasn't his ability on the football field," Sherman said. "It was he's too short. Obviously, he's tall enough to make

it to the Super Bowl twice. There are some 6'5"
quarterbacks that are home right now."

Chapter 6: Wilson's Personal Life

Family

While many factors contributed to Russell Wilson's
success, probably one of the greatest influences was his
entire family. He grew up in a sports-craving competitive
family, who were not only talented in sports, but also
excelled in their academics and careers as well.

Harrison B. Wilson, Jr. – Russell Wilson's Grandfather

The family sports tree started with Russell Wilson's
grandfather, Harrison B. Wilson, Jr. He was born on April
21, 1925. While attending Kentucky State University,
Harrison was a star athlete in basketball, football, baseball,
and even track. Not only was he competitive in sports, but
he also graduated with honors.

Harrison Wilson began his professional career as a
basketball coach at Jackson State University. Between
1951 and 1967, Harrison served as head basketball coach.

From 1960 to 1967, he was also the chairman of the Department of Health and Physical Education. He had an outstanding coaching career, as his team had a record of 340 wins and only 72 losses. In 1975, Harrison became president of Norfolk State University. He was able to lead the entire college to become one of the best colleges in southeastern Virginia. He was known for always wanting to raise the bar for the college, both in athletics and academics.

Harrison Wilson III – Russell Wilson's Father

Russell gives credit to his father, Harrison Wilson III, for being one of the greatest influences in his life. While his father died two years before the Seahawks drafted him, Russell Wilson acknowledges his father for inspiring him toward athletic greatness. Many who knew Russell Wilson's dad say that they can see Harrison's spirit in his son – someone who takes great pride and dedication in achieving greatness. They say that they can see not only Harrison's athleticism, but also his morals and mannerisms. Harrison Wilson III not only taught all of his children how they should play the sport, but he often discussed how to behave as a professional athlete. He told them how they should properly dress for press conferences—even long before Russell had his first experience talking with the media. No doubt, Russell has a great amount of gratitude for his deceased father, who is still alive in his spirit today.

Russell Wilson's father, just like his grandfather, excelled both in academics and sports. During college, he played football and baseball at Dartmouth College. He continued in his academics, attending law school at the University of Virginia. He even became the president of the law school.

After obtaining his law degree, Harrison decided to take his love for sports to the next level and tried out for the San Diego Chargers during their training camp as a wide receiver. While he had the goal of becoming a professional athlete, he deferred his ambition and obtained his law degree out of respect for his father. While he did play during the preseason with the Chargers in 1980, they later decided to let him go.

However, because he obtained a law degree, he became a successful lawyer instead of becoming a professional athlete. While he never realized his dream of playing football professionally, it was obvious his son would become this manifestation. Harrison taught Russell everything he knew about how to excel in sports.

For Russell Wilson, there is simply nobody he can thank more than his father for giving him the ambition toward becoming one of the greatest quarterbacks of his era. Because of this, even though his father died, he thinks about his father every time he puts on a uniform and attempt to lead his team to victory as the starting quarterback for the Seattle Seahawks.

Russell Wilson's Siblings

Russell also has one brother and sister, and they were both athletes as well. Russell often played football and other sports with his brother Harry, Harrison Wilson IV, who was an inspiration that helped him become the competitive player he is today. Because his brother was three years older, Russell often had the challenge of trying to compete against his height and strength advantages. Regardless of being an older brother and having these advantages, Harry never cut his little brother any slack. For Russell, this made him more determined to win, which contributed toward his competitive spirit today.

Harry went on to play college football and baseball at the University of Richmond. However, unlike Russell, he never played professionally. Incidentally, one other person who has made it big in sports is Russell's sister, Anna Wilson.

Anna graduated from Collegiate High School. She is considered one of the nation's top women's basketball players. Much like Russell, Anna grew up loving sports because of her family. Being the youngest sibling, Anna was able to see her two older brothers excel in sports, which gave her the drive to be competitive as well. Her high-level basketball skills have made her one of the most sought-after women's basketball players in the United States, and colleges throughout the 50 states tried hard to recruit her. She is currently playing as a 5'8" point guard. She has many of the same characteristics that Russell possesses, which were undoubtedly contributed by her entire family.

While women's sports are not as visible as male sports, one thing is certain, and that is that Anna Wilson is going places, just as her older brother Russell has. She has already committed to play for the Stanford Cardinal women's basketball team. She has it made: She will not only be a star player, but will also obtain one of the best college educations in the country.

Conclusion

One thing is for sure: without the support and competitive spirit of Russell Wilson's family, he would not be where he is today. This is especially true because even though he is one of the shortest NFL quarterbacks today, he still can play just as competitively as all of the other NFL quarterbacks that are taller than him, even by five inches or more.

Many question whether his athleticism is due to having athletic genes in the family or because his family practically bred him into playing sports. Or maybe it is simply a combination of the two. Whatever the case may be, Russell Wilson hails from a family that truly inspired him to become the greatest he can be.

Wilson's Divorce

Most celebrities are the subjects of juicy rumors featured on tabloids, and Russell Wilson is no exception. The most popular rumor involving Russell Wilson has to do with his ex-wife, Ashton Meem.

Wilson and Ashton's romance began as "high school love," and they met in 2006 while he was the quarterback superstar at Collegiate High School. Ashton was attending St. Catherine's High School, which is also located in Richmond, VA. Their romance continued through high school, and all the way through college.

To keep their love kindled, Ashton Meem chased Wilson to three different colleges. While Ashton went away to college in Georgia, Wilson got a scholarship to play football at North Carolina State University. Ashton broke up with her boyfriend soon after that, and she transferred to North Carolina State. Then she continued to follow Wilson, transferring to Wisconsin when he decided to part ways with North Carolina State. They continued their relationship throughout college.

Soon after college, Wilson popped the question and asked Meem to marry him by placing the message, "Hey Mom, Dad has a question to ask you" on their beagle's dog tag. They then got married in 2012, just before the Seattle Seahawks drafted Wilson.

However, their relationship before marriage lasted longer than the marriage itself. They were married for just two years before filing for divorce in 2014. It was during their time of divorce when the relationship rumors started kicking in.

Because of Russell Wilson's divorce, rumors started to circulate. Rumormongers believed Ashton Meem was having an affair with the Seahawks' wide receiver Golden Tate. However, Golden Tate bluntly stated that all of these allegations were simply not true, and he has denied having any romantic relationship with Ashton.

But how did all of these rumors start? One instance occurred when Golden Tate and Percy Harvin, who were both wide receivers for the Seahawks at the time, got into an altercation in the locker room prior to the 2014 Super

Bowl. Soon, social media started the frenzy, circulating a story that the altercation started with Harvin confronting Golden Tate for having an affair with Russell Wilson's wife.

Another reason these rumors spread was because Golden Tate's girlfriend and Ashton Meem are close friends. Therefore, the idea that there were close ties with everyone elevated the rumors even more.

As mentioned, Golden Tate completely denied all allegations and said that people should not believe everything they hear. However, Russell Wilson never really addressed this allegation publicly, which made some individuals feel that the rumors could potentially be true.

During an interview with TMZ, Golden Tate expressed his anger with Russell Wilson because he should have also told the public that the affair allegations were false. To this day, Tate denies that these allegations were true. Additionally, there has never been any evidence that an affair ever occurred, other than the simple rumors that came about through social media.

Tate wrote a lengthy blog about his stance on the alleged affair with Meem on The Cauldron website on January 16, 2015. At the time, he already left the Seattle Seahawks. He was already a member of the Detroit Lions.

"I did not have an affair with Russell Wilson's wife," Tate reiterated. "Nor did I have anything to do with his divorce. This is laughable for anyone who knows us. His ex-wife, Ashton, is still best friends with my girlfriend. Russell and I were good friends when I was in Seattle, on and off the field – he knows the rumors about me were unfounded, damaging to my reputation, and an attack on my character. Anyone who circulated that rumor was just plain irresponsible."

However, Golden Tate did admit that he had an altercation with Percy Harvin, but did not divulge any details. Considering that they were just about to compete in the Super Bowl, which is the most-watched event on television in the United States, it is very probable that the altercation was over something else. Also, Percy has been known to have feuds with other players in the past, so the altercation between Golden and Percy should not have been that surprising.

"There was also a social media frenzy concerning me and Percy Harvin," Tate continued in his The Cauldron blog. "To set the record straight, I was not punched by Percy during Super Bowl week last year, nor did I have a black eye, as was speculated on by various Internet reports. I even saw a photo of my face that was Photoshopped with a mark on it! Percy and I did have a confrontation, yes, but no punches were thrown, and it certainly never rose to the level that was erroneously reported by certain outlets. I highly respect his level of play. He's one of the best in the game!"

Being in the public spotlight, Russell Wilson realized that he would probably have to make a statement about his divorce. He admitted that he was filing for divorce, requested everyone to pray for the situation, and then mentioned that he had "no further comment" about the situation. Some of the secrecy about the divorce probably helped to motivate the rumors. However, one must consider that divorce is a fragile event for anyone –

whether they are in the public's eye or not, and most would not want to discuss such a difficult situation.

Many athletes get married and divorce, so this is not something uncommon. However, why did this become such a huge social media frenzy? It probably had to do with the fact that this was seen as an adorable "high school sweetheart" relationship that somehow went sour.

Russell's Religious Convictions

There are many characteristics that make up a champion quarterback. One undoubtedly is having extreme athleticism. Other important characteristics include being extremely disciplined, being extremely intelligent, and being a charismatic leader. However, one characteristic that Russell Wilson possesses that not all NFL quarterbacks have is a strong religious conviction.

During many press conferences, Wilson will thank his God for the win. Wilson undoubtedly shares his religious beliefs on his sleeve, and he is not shy or ashamed to do so.

Sometimes, having a strong religious belief can benefit an athlete, and can also hinder one's ability. However, for

Russell Wilson, it seems to work toward his interest. Having a strong religious belief has helped Wilson as an NFL quarterback. It gives him a strong gratitude for the talent and surrounding people that he believes his God has placed in his life. His religious faith also gives him the belief that being extremely disciplined will help him succeed, as well as the realization that, without God, he could have gone in the wrong direction.

Russell Wilson claims that he invited Jesus into his heart at the young age of 14. He recalls, in a documentary entitled *"The Making of a Champion,"* that God came to him in a dream in which his father died. Then Jesus came to Wilson and told him that he needed to find out more about Jesus.

Wilson says that he went to church the following Sunday and accepted Christ into his heart. And since then, he believes that he became an entirely different person. He claimed that before that day that he would beat up other kids, and would even "bite them." However, Wilson believes that since he has accepted Jesus into his heart, he was able to have the discipline and direction toward becoming the great athlete he is today.

The Making of a Champion also explains how many of the Seattle Seahawks players and coaches are deeply religious, and how it contributes toward their hard work and dedication to being the great team that they are. Although the documentary shows that the Seahawks are a "team of believers," they still welcome any player with any belief.

Russell Wilson also explains in the documentary how he was able to accomplish everything he set his heart to, even though many said he would not be able to do it. He feels that God has gifted him with an amazing ability to throw the football, even though he is only 5'11". Wilson believes that, through the power of God, he was able to show all critics that he was capable of still being one of the greatest quarterbacks of all time, even with such a height disadvantage.

However, one major charge that many critics bring against the documentary is that it might not make some players feel welcome to join the team if they do not hold the same Christian beliefs and values. Many also believe that it could ultimately send a wrong message about the NFL, that their intentions should not be for the purpose of spreading

Christianity. It also could potentially cross the fine line between religion and playing the sport of football.

Regardless, Russell Wilson is grateful to be part of a team that has a high set of Christian values and beliefs. Ultimately, many critics probably cannot doubt that having a quarterback leader with strong Christian beliefs can help the entire team propel. A perfect example to prove this is the life of Tim Tebow.

When the Denver Broncos drafted Tim Tebow in 2010, one thing he always made evident was his religious belief. His parents were missionaries and he was born in the Philippines, the country his parents lived in to spread the Gospel. Many doubted Tebow's ability to be an NFL quarterback, especially because he could not throw the football very well.

However, regardless of what many critics stated, Tim Tebow had an uncanny ability to consistently carry his team to victory. He set a record by throwing the longest overtime touchdown pass in NFL playoff history, and twice in a four-game stretch he led the Denver Broncos to victory from a deficit of 13 or more points. Many believe that this came from the energy that spread to both Denver Broncos' defense and offense. It may not have been "God" himself that provided the victory, but some believe it was the fact that Tim Tebow's strong faith and beliefs were so evident that he was able to spread his faith and optimism onto practically every player of the Broncos.

To this very day, Wilson's Christian convictions remain very strong.

Wilson met former San Diego Chargers defensive back Miles McPherson at a prayer breakfast before the Wisconsin Badgers' Rose Bowl game against the Oregon Ducks in 2012. McPherson is now the lead pastor at The Rock Church in San Diego. Wilson made a strong impression on McPherson. The two men met once again at a Pro Athletes Outreach conference. They have been close ever since.

McPherson even does chapel service for the Seahawks when they are in San Diego. One summer, the pastor invited Wilson to his church. He wanted to interview the

Seattle Seahawks quarterback in front of his congregation. Wilson accepted.

The big day came. Wilson took a selfie with McPherson and the group before sitting on an armchair. Wilson told everyone present Jesus Christ spoke to him as soon as he left the field after he threw that ill-fated interception in Super Bowl XLIX against the New England Patriots. He said God's reason for the interception was for Wilson to show how he'd compose himself in such a trying situation.

"There's a silver lining," Wilson proclaimed. "Jesus is so amazing."

He also told the San Diego pastor he knew he would end up with girlfriend in R& B singer Ciara. Wilson claimed God's reason for them becoming a couple was for him to lead her to Christ. Because of this, they were to practice abstinence before they got married.

"He has anointed both of us," Wilson told the congregation. "He has called us to do something miraculous, something special."

Wilson is consistent with his Christian convictions on and off the field. For instance, he kneels and prays with other teammates after a Seahawks victory. He also points to the sky whenever Seattle comes up with an amazing play. He even singled out John 3:30 ("He must increase, but I must decrease.") as his Bible verse for the year 2015 on Twitter.

So, leaving religion aside, Russell Wilson's strong leadership role could simply be because he has such a strong belief in doing his best, and it spreads through the entire team. It can't be denied that, despite being the current shortest starting quarterback in the NFL, Wilson led the Seahawks to winning the Super Bowl in only his second year.

Relationship with Ciara

Russell Wilson publicly admitted he's dating R&B singer Ciara (real name: Ciara Princess Harris) when Pastor Miles McPherson of The Rock church in San Diego interviewed him in July 2015.

"I do have a girlfriend, yes," Wilson said. "She's a sweetheart."

The Seattle Seahawks quarterback then referred to a photo of himself and his girlfriend on the screen.

"Yeah, that's my girlfriend," Wilson continued. "She's everything you could ever want, honestly…I met her five, six months ago. The funny thing is, I told somebody that's the girl I want to be with before I even meet her…If there's a 10, she's a 15."

Ciara has a son with her ex-boyfriend, rapper Future.

Wilson told McPherson's congregation that both of them have had their share of heartaches. He even referred to his past marriage with Ashton Meem, although he didn't mention her name.

Wilson then mentioned he and Ciara are abstaining from sex before they get married. However, he did insinuate it wasn't easy.

"I ain't going to lie to you all now," Wilson joked. "I need you all to pray for us."

For her part, Ciara backed up Wilson on how difficult it can be. In February 2016, she gave *Cosmopolitan* magazine an update on how she and Wilson have been doing as far as their vow of abstinence is concerned.

"It's going pretty good," Ciara remarked. "We're hanging in there. I'm not gonna lie. I'm human, so it is not easy, especially when I look at him and I think he is the most beautiful thing I've ever seen–that I've ever laid my eyes on, to be honest. I'm like, 'Look the other way! Look the other way!'"

Ironically, Ciara told *People* magazine a week or so later that deciding to abstain from sex before marriage wasn't a hard decision.

"No, it's not hard at all," she said. "He's an awesome guy and a very confident guy. Just like I feel I'm a woman that knows what I want, he's a man who knows what he wants."

Ciara added she enjoys the transparency she and Wilson practice in their relationship.

"It's just a fun new chapter in life for me," she said. "We talk about everything, and I think that's what you should be able to do as people and partners in a relationship. So, that's what makes it really beautiful."

Wilson has expressed his admiration for Ciara on social media. He posted on Instagram a photo in which he wore a designer suit by Phillip Plein while he was next to his lady love at the Black Entertainment Television awards in 2015. Ciara did a dance number that paid tribute to Janet Jackson.

Wilson also posted a photo of himself and Ciara dancing to the music of Prince and Stevie Wonder at the White House. She even went with him when he visited a local children's hospital.

Wilson and Ciara have taken their relationship to the next level–they are now officially engaged.

Ciara's representative reveals that the Seahawks quarterback took her on a surprise romantic holiday after Paris Fashion Week. They played a game of "travel roulette" where he showed her a list of 30 possible destinations. He then asked her where they were going. To her amazement, they went to Seychelles in East Africa. They stayed at the North Island resort.

Many high-profile couples, such as Prince William and Princess Kate, Brad Pitt and Angelina Jolie, and David and Victoria Beckham have gone on vacation there. Now, Russell Wilson and Ciara are officially part of that exclusive list.

The representative then said Wilson proposed to Ciara at the "Honeymoon Beach" in North Island.

"She said yes," Wilson said in a short video he tweeted.

"Since Day 1 knew you were the one. No greater feeling," he wrote on Twitter.

"God Is Good!" Ciara tweeted. "Grateful for you @DangRussWilson. You Are Heaven Sent. I'm Looking Forward To Spending Forever With You."

Wilson and Ciara have yet to mention any plans for their wedding. One thing is for sure: Both of them will enjoy a beautiful marriage. Seahawks fans–and NFL fans for that matter–hope they will have many children together. For Russell Wilson, he now has a Super Bowl ring and the woman of his dreams. It certainly does not get any better than that.

Chapter 7: Russell's Dual Professional Careers

Russell Wilson has had tremendous success as the Seattle Seahawks' first-string quarterback. However, this is not Wilson's only desire: he also wants to become a professional baseball player.

Wilson always loved baseball and has already had some level of success playing the sport professionally. While playing second base in college, he attended the Colorado Rockies' farm system from 2010 to 2011 when he became a fourth-round draft choice. During his minor-league career, he had a .293 batting average. He hit 9 home runs in 93 games.

Currently, the Texas Rangers have shown interest in Russell Wilson playing for them, and they even invited him to their training camp. Wilson showed very high interest in playing for the Rangers, as he still desires to be a professional baseball player.

However, the question comes down to whether he will have the time and energy to engage in two demanding sports. While it is true that other athletes were able to play dual sports, most notably Deion Sanders and Bo Jackson, Russell Wilson has a considerably more important position in the NFL, being a first-string quarterback. As a quarterback, he has a tremendous amount of responsibility.

Another major consideration for taking on dual sports is the fact that it can dramatically increase chances of getting injured. Holding such a huge role as the Seahawks' starting quarterback, Wilson's interest does not excite the team players and the franchise owners and managers very much, as they want him to focus solely on his position as a starting quarterback.

Regardless of these risks, Russell Wilson is highly motivated to play both sports. In fact, the Texas Rangers acquired his rights via the Rule 5 draft in December of 2013.

Three months later, Wilson suited up for the Rangers in a Cactus League game against the Cleveland Indians. During warm-ups, he took ground balls and practiced double-play drills. Wilson never played in the game. The Indians won, 6-5.

Wilson was all smiles when he saw himself sharing the same locker room with the Rangers players. He considered it to be an honor. He even said he watches baseball regularly. All in all, he considered spring training with the Rangers as "an unbelievable experience."

Former Rangers outfielder Alex Rios said he admired Wilson's drive and determination.

"His desire to win, it's something that's noticeable," Rios said. "And his dedication to what he does makes him what he is. He's a champion, and I believe that if every single one of us gets the same attitude, we'll be able to achieve many things on the field."

Former Texas manager Ron Washington was just as impressed with Wilson. He thought Wilson has a great physique and mindset for baseball.

"If he continued to work and got the repetition (in baseball)," Washington said, "he could probably be as good as he is a football player."

After spring training with the Rangers, they are highly interested in negotiating a contract with him.

In April of 2015, Wilson didn't deny that he's always dreamed of becoming a dual-sport athlete like Sanders and Jackson.

"I never want to kill the dream of playing two sports," he said. "I would honestly play two sports…That's why the Texas Rangers got my rights. They want me to play. (Rangers general manager) Jon Daniels wants me to play. We were talking about it the other day."

Sanders tried to convince Wilson he should play baseball again a year earlier. Despite his dream of returning to the diamond, he said even back then the Seahawks were his priority.

For his part, Daniels told the media that the Rangers have no plans of luring Wilson away from the Seahawks.

"Russell has the competitiveness and work ethic to where he'd have a shot if he committed to baseball," Daniels said. "Obviously, he's got a pretty good thing going on with the Seahawks, and we're not going to get in the way of that. Playing quarterback is more intensive than the positions of other guys who have attempted to play both sports."

One of the biggest challenges Russell Wilson will have to consider for this has to do with his future football contracts. If he wants to stay in high demand for NFL future contracts, then he would probably need to reconsider playing baseball. The Seattle Seahawks, as well as any other NFL team that may consider hiring him as their quarterback, want him to focus his time and energy playing solely as a quarterback.

In either case, it seems highly unlikely that Russell Wilson will have the Seattle Seahawks' approval to commit to playing baseball and being their quarterback at the same time. Simply put, the strains of being a quarterback are way too overwhelming. Therefore, if he wanted to commit to baseball, he would probably have to give up playing football–and that is highly improbable. He simply is too gifted to leave the NFL and would be giving up too much to do so.

Conclusion

There is no doubt that Russell Wilson is a great athlete. There are probably many factors that contribute toward this. First of all, he grew up with a family that simply loved to compete in sports and life in general. As previously mentioned, Russell Wilson attributes his greatness to his father, who taught him everything he needed to know about football and sports, and was always there to cheer him on.

From the day he started playing sports with his older brother, all the way to winning the Super Bowl in the NFL, Russell Wilson always kept a drive toward being the best he could be. His relentless commitment toward success led him to become the great NFL quarterback that he is today. Even though many recognize Wilson as a highly talented quarterback, he has also shown that he could even potentially become a professional baseball player. While he has a deep desire to play professional baseball someday, his commitment toward being one of the greatest quarterbacks in NFL history may keep him from fulfilling this dream. At this point, we can only wait and see what choices Wilson will make.

Russell Wilson was criticized and doubted as to his ability to play as a quarterback in professional football. It had absolutely nothing to do with his stats, his leadership ability, or his athleticism. It was simply due to his height.

Most analysts would have never thought Russell Wilson, at only 5'11", would be able to accomplish what he already has. Many of his critics assumed he would have a better chance if he played another sport, like baseball, or that he would have been better off playing a different position than quarterback.

But Russell Wilson's height was never a determining factor for him. In fact, it just gave him more motivation to show everyone who questioned his capabilities that they were completely wrong. In fact, he thrives on criticism. He wants to prove to everyone that he is the all-time greatest quarterback in NFL history. Despite being a 75th overall pick with a four-year rookie contract worth $2.9 million with the Seattle Seahawks, Wilson never let up on his commitment. Despite that, he showed that he has everything it takes to become a great quarterback. He knew that if Drew Brees, who is only one inch taller than him, was capable of becoming a great quarterback, he would be able to accomplish his dream of playing as a starting quarterback as well.

Wilson has played only four seasons in the NFL. He made himself a highly-touted quarterback after his first season playing with the Seahawks. After signing a lucrative, four-year contract extension worth $87.6 million in 2015, he can now be mentioned as one of the NFL's elite quarterbacks. Think Tom Brady, Drew Brees, Eli Manning, Ben Roethlisberger, and Joe Flacco.

But there is one question that remains, and that is: What else can Russell Wilson accomplish? He has played only three regular seasons in the NFL, and he is not even close to reaching his prime yet. Sports enthusiasts can only imagine what will become of Wilson's NFL career as a quarterback, and they are highly excited about the history he will make. He already has record-breaking completion percentages and total passing yards, and he has accomplished all this in just four seasons.

Anyone who has studied and learned about Russell Wilson should know one thing about him: without a shadow of a doubt, he always thrives toward excellence. This means that he will most likely become a better quarterback and a better leader. Many would say that Russell Wilson is probably one of the most competitive NFL quarterbacks of all time. With the way things are going, the Seahawks will most likely end up winning multiple Super Bowls. This might be mere speculation, but most would agree that Wilson's chances of winning more titles in the future are very good.

In addition to being an excellent quarterback, Russell Wilson is also a tremendous role model. He holds extremely high Christian values, which helps him set a good example to everyone watching him. He does not just want to go down as the all-time greatest quarterback; he also wants to show others how great his God is to him. One way he demonstrates this is by proving that he could be a great quarterback, even though many doubted him because of his height disadvantage. Nonetheless, he likes to share his belief that God is a major reason that he is so successful. Many would consider Russell Wilson as an outstanding all-around person—not only is he a great athlete, but he is definitely a great role model for everyone who looks up to him.

Final Word/About the Author

I was born and raised in Norwalk, Connecticut. Growing up, I could often be found spending many nights watching basketball, soccer, and football matches with my father in the family living room. I love sports and everything that sports can embody. I believe that sports are one of most genuine forms of competition, heart, and determination. I write my works to learn more about influential athletes in the hopes that from my writing, you the reader can walk away inspired to put in an equal if not greater amount of hard work and perseverance to pursue your goals. If you enjoyed *Russell Wilson: The Inspiring Story of One of Football's Greatest Quarterbacks,* please leave a review! Also, you can read more of my works on *Colin Kaepernick, Aaron Rodgers, Peyton Manning, Tom Brady, Michael Jordan, LeBron James, Kyrie Irving, Klay Thompson, Stephen Curry, Kevin Durant, Russell Westbrook, Anthony Davis, Chris Paul, Blake Griffin, Kobe Bryant, Joakim Noah, Scottie Pippen, Carmelo Anthony, Kevin Love, Grant Hill, Tracy McGrady, Vince Carter, Patrick Ewing, Karl Malone, Tony Parker, Allen*

Iverson, Hakeem Olajuwon, Reggie Miller, Michael Carter-Williams, John Wall, James Harden, Tim Duncan, Steve Nash, Pau Gasol, Marc Gasol, Jimmy Butler, Dirk Nowitzki, Draymond Green, Pete Maravich, Kawhi Leonard, Dwyane Wade, Ray Allen and Paul George in the Kindle Store. If you love basketball, check out my website at claytongeoffreys.com to join my exclusive list where I let you know about my latest books and give you lots of goodies.

Like what you read? Please leave a review!

I write because I love sharing the stories of influential people like Russell Wilson with fantastic readers like you. My readers inspire me to write more so please do not hesitate to let me know what you thought by leaving a review! If you love books on life, basketball, or productivity, check out my website at claytongeoffreys.com to join my exclusive list where I let you know about my latest books. Aside from being the first to hear about my latest releases, you can also download a free copy of *33 Life Lessons: Success Principles, Career Advice & Habits of Successful People*. See you there!

Clayton

References

1. "Most TD Passes First 2 Seasons." ESPN.com. 3 December 2013. Web.

2. "Russell Wilson Game-By-Game Stats." ESPN.com. Web.

3. Gittings, Paul. "Seattle Seahawks Win Super Bowl for First Time In Its History." CNN. 7 February 2014. Web.

4. "Russell Wilson Biography." Bio.com. March 6, 2016. Web.

5. "Russell Wilson: I Found God When Jesus Came to Me In A Dream At 14." CBS Seattle. Web.

6. Corbett, Jim. "Seahawks' Russell Wilson Channels Father's Influence as Player, Leader." *USA Today Sports*. 10 January 2015. Web.

7. O'Neil, Danny. "Russell Wilson Defied All Odds to Become The Talk of the NFL." *The Seattle Times*. 22 December 2012. Web.

8. Thomas, Linda. "The Childhood, Family and Faith Behind Seahawk Russell Wilson." MyNorthwest.com. 10 January 2013. Web.

9. Wilson, Russell. "Let's Talk About It." The PlayersTribune.com. 2 October 2014. Web.

10. Steele, David. "Want to Know Russell Wilson? First, Learn About His Father." *Sporting News*. 17 January 2014. Web.

11. Spelman, Jeff. "QB Russell Wilson's First Hometown: Cincinnati." Youthletic.com. Web.

12. Pilkington, Taylor. "Virginia's Favorite QB." Virginia Living. 2 September 2014. Web.

13. Ringer, Sandy. "Russell Wilson's Sister, Anna, Makes Her Own Name as a Bellevue High Basketball Star." *The Seattle Times*. 14 January 2016. Web.

14. Almond, Elliott. "Seattle Quarterback Russell Wilson's Sister Signs With Stanford." *San Jose Mercury News*. 11 November 2015. Web.

15. Kirpalani, Sanjay. "The College Recruitment of Russell Wilson." Bleacher Report. 22 October 2015. Web

16. Utley, Arthur. "Russell Wilson: Times-Dispatch Player of the Year 2005." *The Richmond Times- Dispatch*. 20 December 2005. Web.

17. Freeman, Vernon Jr. "Collegiate School Receives Commemorative Golden Football in Honor of Russell Wilson." WTVR.com. 15 January 2016. Web.

18. King, Michael. "Meet Russell Wilson's High School Coach." King5.com. 22 January 2015. Web.

19. Giglio, Joe. "Russell Wilson Passes Along Tips, Smiles at His NC State Football Camp." *The News & Observer*. 23 June 2015. Web.

20. "Russell Wilson Was Once in the Colorado Rockies Organization." CBS Denver. 28 January 2014. Web.

21. Dinich, Heather. "O'Brien on Russell Wilson: 'We're Good.'" ESPN. 24 January 2014. Web

22. University of Wisconsin School of Education. "Ex-Badger Wilson Called 'NFL's Higher Education Most Valuable Player.'" education.wisconsin.edu. 3 February 2014. Web

23. Cohen, Ben. "How Wisconsin Imported a Quarterback." *The Wall Street Journal*. 21 October 2011. Web.

24. Kelly, Danny. "Flashback: Bret Bielema Talks Russell Wilson." www.Fieldgulls.com. 23 July 2013. Web.

25. "Russell Wilson Shines in Wisconsin Debut as Badgers Roll Over UNLV." ESPN.com. 2 September 2011. Web.

26. Friedell, Dan. "How Good Was Russell Wilson at Baseball?" ESPN. 9 January 2013. Web.

27. "Michigan St. Shocks Wisconsin With Hail Mary From Kirk Cousins to Kirk Nichol." ESPN.com. 20 October 2012. Web.

143

28. "Last-Minute Touchdown Toss Helps Buckeyes Top Badgers." ESPN.com. 20 October 2011. Web.

29. Arthur, Kenneth. "Russell Wilson, NFL Draft Prospect: The Complete History of Wilson's Run From Rose Bowl to Draft Day." 24 April 2014. Web.

30. Fowler, Jeremy. "Russell Wilson Set Stage For Stardom With 'Take Charge' Senior Bowl Performance." ESPN. 16 January 2015. Web.

31. "Russell Wilson Combine Player Profile." NFL.com. February 2012. Web.

32. Bien, Louis, "2012 NFL Combine Results: Robert Griffin III Fastest in 40-Yard Dash Among Quarterbacks." SBNation.com. 26 February 2012. Web.

33. Eaton, Nick. "Seahawks Take Quarterback Russell Wilson in Third Round of NFL Draft." *The Seattle Post-Intelligencer*. 27 April 2012. Web.

34. "Seattle Seahawks Rookie Russell Wilson Debuts vs. Arizona Cardinals." The Associated Press. 22 May 2013. Web.

35. Kevin Kolb Replaces Hurt John Skelton, Helps Cards by Seahawks." ESPN.com. 10 September 2012. Web.

36. Farnsworth, Clare. "Was 2012 Defense Best in Franchise History?" Seahawks.com. 15 February 2013. Web.

37. "Redskins Lose Lead, Robert Griffin III as Seahawks Prevail." ESPN.com. 7 Jan. 2013. Web.

38. "Matt Bryant's Late FG Stuns Seahawks, Lifts Falcons to Playoff Win." ESPN.com. 14 January 2013. Web.

39. Farnsworth, Clare. "Russell Wilson Named NFL.com Rookie of the Year." Seahawks.com. 2 February 2013. Web.

40. "Cards Snap Seahawks' 14-Game Home Winning Streak." Sportsnetwork.com (via FoxNews.com). 22 December 2013. Web.

41. "NFL Player Passing Statistics – 2013." ESPN.com. Web.

42. "NFL Total Defense Statistics – 2013." ESPN.com. Web.

43. "NFL Player Receiving Statistics – 2013." ESPN.com. Web.

44. "Marshawn Lynch, Seahawks Top Saints To Reach NFC Title Game." ESPN.com. 12 January 2014. Web.

45. "Seahawks Hold Off 49ers' Late Rally, Advance to Super Bowl." ESPN.com. 19 January 2014. Web.

46. "Box Score – San Francisco 49ers vs. Seattle Seahawks." FootballDB.com. 19 January 2014. Web.

47. Hunt, Donald. "Doug Williams Started the Super Bowl Trail for Black QBs." *The Philadelphia Tribune*. 2 February 2016. Web.

48. "Seattle Seahawks' D Dominates Manning, Denver Broncos to Win Super Bowl." The Associated Press (via NFL.com). 2 February 2014. Web.

49. "Seahawks vs. Broncos - Box Score – February 2, 2014 – ESPN." ESPN.com. 2 February 2014. Web.

50. "Super Bowl XLVIII 2013 Postseason Media Guide." Wordpress.com. Web.

51. Moser, Josh. "Broncos Fall Short in OT Against Seahawks." 9News.com. 21 September 2014. Web

52. "Russell Wilson Powers Seahawks Past Redskins." ESPN.com. 7 October 2014. Web.

53. "Defense Propels Seattle to Top of NFC West." The Associated Press (via NFL.com). 21 December 2014. Web.

54. "Panthers Bury Cardinals Behind Cam Newton, Historic Effort on Defense." ESPN.com. 4 January 2015. Web.

145

55. "Russell Wilson, Kam Chancellor Star as Seahawks Roll into Title Game." ESPN.com. 11 January 2015. Web.

56. "Seahawks Rally to Stun Packers in OT, Clinch Return Trip to Super Bowl." ESPN.com. 19 January 2015. Web.

57. "Malcolm Butler's Goal-Line Interception Gives Pats Super Bowl XLIX Title." ESPN.com. 2 February 2015. Web.

58. Condotta, Bob. "Post-Game Quotes From Seattle Quarterback Russell Wilson." *The Seattle Times*. 2 February 2015. Web.

59. Condotta, Bob. "Seahawks Agree to Contract Extension With Quarterback Russell Wilson." *The Seattle Times*. 31 July 2015. Web.

60. "Wilson's 5 TDs Lead Seattle Past Pittsburgh 39-30." ESPN.com. 30 November 2015. Web.

61. Kapadia, Sheil. "Russell Wilson Sets Single-Season Team Marks For Passing Yards, TD Throws." ESPN.com. 3 January 2016. Web.

62. Kapadia, Sheil. "Five Numbers Behind Russell Wilson's Historic Season." ESPN.com. 4 January 2016. Web.

63. Kelly, Danny. "Seahawks Regular Season Summary Summary From Pro Football Focus." Fieldgulls.com. 8 January 2016. Web.

64. "Seahawks Survive, Advance After Hooked FG." ESPN.com. 10 January 2016. Web.

65. "NFL Team Total Defense Statistics – 2015." ESPN.com. Web.

66. "Panthers Hold Off Seahawks, Advance to NFC Title Game." ESPN.com. Web.

67. Cochran, Amanda. "Seahawks Quarterback Russell Wilson: "My Height Doesn't Define My Skill Set." CBS News. 3 February 2014. Web.

68. Blount, Terry. "Seahawks Never Doubt Russell Wilson's Leadership." ESPN.com. 26 January 2015. Web.

146

69. Brodesser-Akner, Taffy. "The Higher Power of Russell Wilson." *ESPN the Magazine*. 24 December 2015. Web.

70. Tate, Golden. "Silence Isn't Golden." TheCauldron.SI.com. 16 January 2015. Web.

71. Rothman, Michael. "Inside Seahawks QB Russell Wilson and Ciara's Relationship." ABC News. 7 July 2015. Web.

72. Manning, Charles. "Ciara Reveals What Abstinence With Russell Wilson Really Means." *Cosmopolitan* Magazine. 11 February 2016. Web.

73. Randel, Becky. "Ciara Says 'It Wasn't Hard' to Talk About Abstinence With Boyfriend Russell Wilson: 'It's A Fun New Chapter In Life For Me.'" *People* Magazine. 20 February 2016. Web.

74. Chiu, Melody. "Ciara is Engaged to Russell Wilson! All Details on the Surprise Proposal." *People* Magazine. 11 March 2016. Web.

75. Knoblauch, Austin. "Texas Rangers Won't Interfere with Russell Wilson's NFL Career." *The Los Angeles Times*. 19 April 2015. Web.

76. Cassavell, A.J. "Wilson Makes an Impression on Rangers." MLB.com. 3 March 2014. Web.

41729661R00086

Made in the USA
San Bernardino, CA
19 November 2016